WAKING THE
SLEEPING GIANT

Rediscovering the Church
in the book of Acts

ROBERT GRIFFITH

GRACE AND TRUTH PUBLISHING
PO Box 338, Gunnedah NSW 2380 Australia
www.graceandtruthpublishing.com.au

**All Bible quotes are from the New International Version (NIV) expect where
otherwise stated.**

NEW INTERNATIONAL VERSION (NIV), Copyright 1973, 1978 and 1984 by
international Bible Society. Used by permission of Zondervan Publishing House.
All rights reserved.

Other version quotes are from:

AMPLIFIED BIBLE (AMP), Copyright © 1954, 1958, 1962, 1964, 1965, 1987 by
The Lockman Foundation. Used by permission.

ENGLISH STANDARD VERSION (ESV), Copyright © 2001 by Crossway Bibles,
a division of Good News Publishers. Used by permission. All rights reserved.

NEW AMERICAN STANDARD BIBLE (NASB), Copyright © 1960, 1962, 1963, 1968,
1971, 1972, 1973, 1975, 1977, by The Lockman Foundation. Used by permission.

NEW KING JAMES VERSION (NKJV), Copyright © 1979, 1980, 1982, by Thomas
Nelson Inc. Used by permission. All rights reserved.

THE MESSAGE (MSG), by Eugene Peterson, Copyright © 1993, 1994, 1995, 1996,
and 2000. Used by permission of NavPress Publishing Group. All rights reserved.

REVISED STANDARD VERSION (RSV), Copyright © 1973, by Thomas Nelson Inc.
Used by permission. All rights reserved.

Quotes in square brackets are the author's comment.

ISBN 978-0-6486439-6-8

TABLE OF CONTENTS

CHAPTER ONE
Introduction

Thanks for joining me in this journey back to the origins of the Christian faith. In this book we will return to where it all began, to the birth of the church which Jesus promised to build. My primary reference will be *The Acts of the Apostles* - the fifth book in the New Testament. Now I will acknowledge that *'Waking the Sleeping Giant'* may seem like a provocative title, but I believe it is very appropriate at this point in the church's history.

The 'giant' I refer to is of course the church of Jesus Christ. It is a giant, because when we read the New Testament and gain an accurate understanding of what the church really is and learn about the plan and purpose of God in establishing the church, then we should regard the church as the most significant, the most powerful and influential reality in the whole world. From God's perspective, the church is not peripheral to the world; the world is peripheral to the church.

The church which we discover in the New Testament is not only established by the omnipotent Creator of the universe, but it's also empowered by Him on a daily basis through His Spirit, to be the light in a dark world. The church was created to have a global impact - to touch every heart and life on this planet.

That is the church we are introduced to in the book of Acts, but when I look around me today in my nation, I am really forced to conclude that the modern church barely resembles the New Testament church in its structure, methods, priorities, attitude and certainly its impact on the world.

Hence the title of this book: *Waking the Sleeping Giant*, because for all intents and purposes, the church we see in the New Testament fell asleep at some point between Pentecost and today. We are still the same church theologically speaking - for there is only one - and yet our presence and influence in society is at such a low ebb that it should be argued the church really needs to wake up!

It doesn't seem that long ago when political and social leaders in our society would approach the church for an opinion or even advice on matters which impacted communities in a significant way. Not only do they not approach us anymore – now we have to almost knock down doors to be seen or heard. Even if we are given a hearing, very little respect is given to our position for we are now regarded as just another minority group in the society who wants to push our own narrow agenda.

So, what on earth happened? Why are the custodians of the best news any human being could ever hear, marginalised, ignored and treated like a joke? Why do those who are indwelt by the presence of the One Who created this entire universe, seem so powerless against worldly leaders who possess no real power?

How do we wake this sleeping giant? How do we encourage or initiate a re-birth of the true church which we see in the book of Acts? In answer to those questions, I want to say that first and foremost we need sound teaching. We need to go way back and re-discover the truth of our Christian heritage.

We need to put our personal worldview and perspective; all our denominational traditions and our environmental conditioning aside, and take a fresh look at the original church which Jesus Christ birthed and promised to build.

Most of the New Testament will show us what that church was like in those early days, but the Book of Acts is the best place to start if we want to put ourselves back at the birthplace of the church. This sleeping giant will only wake up, rise up and begin to impact the world again when you and I get a firm grasp on what the church really is at its core, and what God's plan and purpose is for His people in the world.

At the end of the earthly ministry of Jesus, He gave us what we call *The Great Commission*. He told us to go into the world and make disciples, teaching them His truth and ushering them all into the glory of the Kingdom rule and reign of Jesus Christ. Following that commission, we then have all the information we will ever need to be able to fulfil our calling.

The book of Acts contains everything we require to embrace the whole plan and purpose of God for the church of Jesus Christ. This is, without doubt, one of the most exciting and helpful books in the entire Bible.

However, it also happens to be one the most confronting and, at times, controversial books in the Bible. It pulls no punches when it comes to power encounters with the supernatural realm and the day-to-day practical ministry of the Spirit, whilst challenging us on every page to get out of our fortress and into the darkness of this broken world with the life-changing message of the gospel of Jesus Christ.

So, under the banner of *Waking the Sleeping Giant,* let's begin this thorough examination of what I believe to be the most relevant and most important part of Scripture for the Christian church if we are seeking to understand the role of the church in the world in the 21st century.

We will move through this slowly so as to allow the Holy Spirit sufficient time to birth in us a life-changing, church-renewing, society-transforming revelation of Christianity at its very best and Christianity as it was always meant to be. Pre-conceptions may be confronted; traditions may be threatened; theology may be challenged; but I believe lives and ministries, and indeed the whole church, will be transformed, empowered and released in the process. The sleeping giant can and must wake up!

I won't be referencing every verse in the book of Acts, but I will be touching on many of the main sections so that we gain a deep and broad understanding of why the Holy Spirit inspired Luke to write this, his second work, and why it was so important to have it included in the Bible.

I really believe that the majority of Christians are neither satisfied with nor completely fulfilled by their church involvement. A growing number of them are fed up with 'playing church.' They are really sick of the political games, factional tensions and the divisions which dominate so much of the church.

They're tired of just coming to services week in and week out while someone up front just turns the handle a few more times, cranking out another service, another sermon, another fix-it-all conference, another evangelistic rally, another small group meeting ... and the list goes on.

There are thousands of people sitting in services each week in this nation who desperately, deep in their souls, want to get to the end of the day, the week, the end of their life and say: *'The Lord has indeed won this battle. Evil has been pushed back. The church that Jesus is building is alive! The kingdom of God s advancing, and I have had the privilege to see it, taste it and be part of it.'*

They want some action! They want to see a church that has the motivation and power to practise what it preaches. They want a church that can stand up and be counted in society. They want it to be the norm where any person can walk into a worship service and genuinely encounter the living, present God Whom we worship. They don't want to be spectators anymore. They want to get onto the field and join the team and be participants in what God is actually doing across the world. When we read the New Testament that's not too much to ask - in fact, that is normal, everyday church life as God always intended.

If you are one of those people, then I believe nothing could help you more in seeing the fulfilment of those desires than for us to study and understand the book of Acts and have the courage to apply what we learn. Peter Wagner once called the book of Acts: *God's Training Manual for the church,* and a growing number of Christian commentators and scholars in recent years have been brave enough to agree with him. Seeing what worked so well 2,000 years ago will directly affect our service to God and our impact on the world today.

Reconnecting to the book of Acts will help bring a life-changing revelation of the nature, plan and purpose of God for us, the church. Now there are thousands of commentaries written on the book of Acts. I think I have at least a ten of the best ones on my bookshelf. But they were not consulted when I wrote this book.

The teaching in this book does not come from commentaries, for I believe a practical, hands-on study of the book of Acts is what is so desperately needed in a church which has more Biblical knowledge and collective wisdom than at any point in history - yet the lost are still lost and the church is still asleep!

History is important and, in some respects, knowing where we have been, can inform and assist us in knowing where to head in the future. However, I am not as interested in the past as I am in the present and the future. Yesterday is now behind us; we have no control over it; we cannot change what happened before today. We should certainly learn from the past, but our focus and energy should be directed to the present and the future.

I therefore do not want us to study the Acts of the Apostles as an historical document, even though it is certainly that. I want us to study the book of Acts in search of the heart of God; the universal plan and purpose of God; and the principles of church life that transcend all barriers of time, language and culture.

If there is universal truth and some practical guidelines in this book which still hold true for the church today, then I want to us to discover them and embrace them afresh. I want us to spend our time mining the gems of wisdom locked within those pages; gems which are intensely practical in helping us fulfil the very important assignment we have all been given.

What is that assignment? Quite simply, we are called to fulfil the great commission; to help God transform all those around us into disciples of Jesus Christ.

Therefore, my desire is to present the truths I have discovered in the book of Acts in a down-to-earth, practical way so that each of us can apply it to our lives and our ministry.

One of my deepest fears as a Bible preacher, teacher and writer is boring my listeners and readers with complicated, technical, albeit accurate material, that no one really cares about. I want us to come to this text with a freshness and a desire to know how the book of Acts impacts the church today and tomorrow.

As much as I respect Biblical commentators, any commentary on the book of Acts that is more than 15 years old is outdated and not very helpful. It may still be very accurate theologically as the writer pursues the nature of God and the purpose of the church for all time. But when it comes to saying what all that means for today's church, it may fail, because in case you haven't noticed, the church and the world today are not the same as they were decades ago when most of the main Bible commentaries we have today were written.

So, I want us to examine the book of Acts through 21st century lenses. I want us to discover the precious gems which have value in our day and our culture and which are relevant to the church as we experience it right now. As we journey through the Biblical text, there will be many issues and principles that surface and I want to take some time to address them if they are relevant to us in our life and ministry today.

However, there are two particular issues which have been the subject of more sermons, books, study and application over the last few decades than could previously be imagined. They are the issues of *power ministry* and *missiology*.

By power ministry I am referring to the supernatural phenomena of healing, deliverance, spiritual warfare, prophecy etc. which we encounter in the book of Acts. This has been referred to as the 'charismatic' dimension of ministry. The theme of power ministry is addressed in the words of Jesus Himself:

> *"But you will receive power when the Holy Spirit comes on you; and you will be my witnesses in Jerusalem, and in all Judea and Samaria, and to the ends of the earth." (Acts 1:8)*

That power is then observed in the ministry of the church on every page that follows. By 'missiology' I refer to the mission of Christ and the purpose of the church. Again, Acts 1:8 sets the scene. It does not say you will receive power from the Holy Spirit for the sake of having power. No, that power is given for a purpose. The word 'power' literally just means 'the ability to do.'

The ability to do what? To be witnesses to Jesus throughout the whole world. We then read on from chapter one and see how the mission of Christ impacts the world around us.

I believe that we have learnt more about power ministries and missiology in this current generation than in all the previous generations combined. The passion for seeing people come to Christ is no longer confined to missionary societies - the whole church is starting to realise that bringing this world to Christ is not a particular ministry of the church, it is actually the ministry of the church and all other ministries must feed into or flow from that mission and purpose.

A desire to know the reality and the power of the Holy Spirit within us and to move in that power and see God perform miracles in and through us is not confined to the Pentecostal arm of the church anymore. Hundreds of thousands of Christians across the world have reconnected with the same Holy Spirit Who gave birth to the church on the day of Pentecost and Who breathed life and power into the followers of Christ as they impacted the whole world with the gospel.

So why is the book of Acts in the Bible? Well, over half the New Testament (56%) is dedicated to explaining the origins and the growth of the Christian faith (i.e., the Gospels and Acts). 38% of the New Testament then deals with the life of existing Christians (i.e., the Epistles). The book of Revelation forms the remaining 6%. This demonstrates that the primary emphasis of the New Testament is directed towards understanding why and how unbelievers can become believers.

Communicating the good news of Jesus Christ to the lost is the major theme of the New Testament. The Gospels and Acts are designed to show us how that task was fulfilled in the past and, in most cases, how it should still be happening today.

The four Gospels record the beginnings of Christianity. Jesus called twelve disciples to Himself at the very start of His earthly ministry. This group soon grew to 70 (Luke 10). By the time we get to Acts, 120 are meeting in the upper room following Jesus' ascension to heaven.

We later read in 1 Corinthians 15 that 500 believers saw the risen Christ all at once - a number that could have been over and above the 120, thereby giving a possible total of 620.

Now some people may wonder why anyone would consider this to be remarkable growth. These are not huge numbers. Well, I know of very few church planters in this nation who have started with no one and seen their church grow to 620 in three years. In fact, statistics show that less than 3% of churches across the western world ever grow past 500, let alone in just three years.

We know the writer of *The Acts of the Apostles* is Luke, the one Paul called the 'beloved physician' and this is the second volume in Luke's two volume series on the origins and expansion of the Christian faith. In simple terms, the Gospel of Luke tells us what Jesus did and the Book of Acts tells us what He now expects His followers to do. Luke was dedicated to spreading the Gospel to the unreached peoples of the world. Luke is, in fact, the only writer in the New Testament (or the whole Bible for that matter) who was not a Jew.

One of the reasons the book of Acts is such a practical book, in spite of being written by a well-educated academic scholar, is that Luke was also a practician. He was a field missionary. He got his hands dirty in the real world of ministry. As we'll see later in our study, Luke writes several sections of this book in the first person ("we") indicating that he drew insights directly from His own experience as he participated in Paul's missionary activities.

With an author possessing the practical, academic and spiritual qualifications of Luke, it is therefore no surprise that in *The Acts of the Apostles,* we have a book which forms a detailed and vitally important training manual for modern Christians.

The major theological framework for our understanding of the book of Acts is the Kingdom of God (or the Kingdom of Heaven). Acts starts with the Kingdom of God and ends with the Kingdom of God. It starts by affirming that prior to His ascension, Jesus spoke to His Apostles about the Kingdom of God.

Then at the end of the book we find the Apostle Paul under house arrest in Rome preaching about the Kingdom of God. So, what is the Kingdom of God? The Kingdom of God is present first and foremost wherever Christ is acknowledged and served as King. 'Kingdom' literally means the 'king's domain.' It is the practical outworking, the visible manifestation of the rule and reign of Jesus Christ. It is not a geographical or geopolitical territory with recognised boundaries. It can't join the United Nations. It's a Kingdom that is not of this world, but nevertheless it is now in this world, thanks to Jesus. It's a spiritual reality but it's also tangible and has visible manifestations.

In one sense the Kingdom of God is also a future reality. There will be a day when the Kingdom to God is the only Kingdom which exists. That will be when Jesus Christ puts an end to all other rule and authority and power. Jesus must reign until He puts all enemies under His feet. The last enemy that will be destroyed is death (1 Corinthians 15). As long as death is with us, the total fulfilment of the Kingdom has not yet come. When it does, we will see a new heaven and a new earth.

Until that day, we live in a world where many enemies of God and His people are still present. Satan, the supreme enemy, is spoken of as 'the God of this age' and the 'prince of the power of the air.' John affirms that the whole world lies under the sway of the wicked one. This language must not be taken lightly - it is used of Satan by those who live this side of the cross. Before Jesus came, things were even worse!

As a result of the strongholds provided through the sin of Adam and Eve, Satan succeeded in usurping the power and control of most human beings and social institutions. He had become so powerful that he could offer Jesus the kingdoms of this world, claiming that: *".. this has been given to me, and I can give it to anyone I want to." (Luke 4:6)*

Interestingly enough, Jesus never denied that Satan had such power. In fact, if Satan did not have that control, the temptation would have been a farce. No wonder Jesus later called him 'the ruler of this world.'

The life, death and resurrection of Jesus radically changed that. When Jesus first came, John the Baptist announced that *"The kingdom of God was at hand."* Jesus later sent His disciples out to preach, *"the Kingdom of God is at hand."*

These statements were actually a declaration of war. According to 1 John 3:8, the purpose of Jesus coming to earth was clear. The reason the Son of God came was *to destroy the works of the devil.* The Kingdom of God invaded the kingdom of Satan. Jesus' death disarmed the principalities and powers and then made a public spectacle of them. Jesus made this declaration of war when He said the following:

> *"From the days of John the Baptist until now, the Kingdom of God is forcefully advancing and forceful men lay hold of it."* (Matthew 11:12)

Jesus was establishing the pattern of things to come. His people would be recruited, mobilised and empowered to move with force against the enemy on behalf of the Kingdom of God. The weapons to conduct this warfare would be spiritual, not natural. In the Lord's prayer, Jesus taught His disciples to pray: *"Your kingdom come, Your will be done on earth as it is in heaven."* Jesus also said: *"My kingdom is not of this world."*

So, what does His kingdom look like? Well, His Kingdom is one where everything is perfect, where there is no sickness or pain or oppression; no demons or dark angels to torment; a kingdom of freedom, love, righteousness and peace. That is the Kingdom Jesus came to usher in. That's why what He did in the Synagogue in His hometown at the outset of His ministry was so significant. By quoting Isaiah 61 and applying the words to Himself, Jesus came to usher in the Kingdom of God by doing six things:

- *Preach the Gospel to the poor*
- *Heal the broken-hearted*
- *Preach deliverance to the captives*
- *Preach recovery of sight to the blind*
- *Set free those who are oppressed*
- *Declare the acceptable year of the Lord's favour*

Therefore, Satan and his kingdom of darkness is delivered a very painful blow every time a sick person is healed; every time a demon is cast out; every time a lost soul finds Jesus; every time a variety of races and cultures live together in love and harmony; every time greed is exposed and overcome; every time families maintain standards of holiness and purity. Satan comes to steal, to kill and to destroy, but Jesus comes that we might have life and have it more abundantly.

When Jesus left earth and returned to the Kingdom of heaven, the task of expanding His Kingdom was left in the hands of His faithful followers, empowered by the Holy Spirit. By using the supernatural power which was now resident within them, they were now able to declare and also to demonstrate the Kingdom of God. They were called to go and make disciples of all nations, baptising them in the name of the Father, the Son and the Holy Spirit, teaching them to observe all things that Jesus had commanded them. (Matthew 28:19-20)

When we turn to the book of Acts, we find more than in any other part of the New Testament, a very clear explanation of how the disciples of Jesus went about implementing their Master's desire that the Kingdom of God be expanded across the whole world. Jesus told them clearly what was about to happen:

> "But you will receive power when the Holy Spirit comes on you; and you will be my witnesses in Jerusalem, and in all Judea and Samaria, and to the ends of the earth." (Acts 1:8)

I look forward to now exploring with you how the early disciples embraced this new power dynamic in their desire to fulfil the mission of Christ.

CHAPTER TWO
Mission Perspectives

As we begin to embrace the truths within the book of Acts, I want us to exercise our heads more than our hearts in this chapter as I make some more general observations about the Book of Acts. I hope to provide insights into cultural anthropology, modern missiology and contemporary sociology, but I plan to present that in a way which is simple, practical and relevant to our current situation.

At the beginning of the book of Acts we see Jesus instructing His eleven Apostles, all of whom were Jews. Later, one hundred and twenty people gathered in the upper room and they too were all Jews. Except for an isolated exception here and there, such as the Samaritan woman at the well and her friends, virtually every one of the early believers was a Jew.

No intentional effort to bring the Gospel to non-Jews is recorded in the Gospels or even in the book of Acts, until chapter 8. There, Philip begins to evangelise the half-breed Samaritans, and later in Acts 10 we see Peter visiting the home of the Gentile Cornelius. But a systematic mission to plant churches among the Gentiles is not recorded until Acts 11, where fifteen years after Pentecost, missionaries from Cyrus and Cyrene travelled to Antioch.

Paul said in Romans 1:16 that the gospel was *"... first for the Jew, then for the Gentile."* Why was this, and why would Jesus say in Matthew 15:24: *"I was sent only to the lost sheep of Israel."* It will not be possible for us to understand the cross-cultural ministry that unfolds in the book of Acts, without first going back to the Gospels to understand how and why Jesus built a nucleus of a hundred and twenty Jews to initiate what has now become more than 2,000 years of transcultural worldwide missions.

Paul had some understandable theological reasons for saying that the Gospel was for the Jews first. He also had a number of personal reasons.

Paul was a Jew - a Hebrew of the Hebrews - who dearly loved his own people. He had such a burden for them that he once said he would give up his own salvation if, by doing so, the Jewish people would follow Jesus as their Messiah (Romans 9:1-5). The covenant which God made with Abraham 4,000 years ago was a clear expression of God's heart for the world. He chose Abraham to be the patriarch of His special people - Israel. God's intention was not only to bless Israel - but much more.

In Genesis 12:3, God said to Abraham: *"... all peoples on earth will be blessed through you."* If the Jewish people had been faithful to God's commission in Old Testament times, history would have probably played out very differently. Even today, many Jews don't understand why history changed so radically for them when Jesus came.

Paul, in his letter to the church in Rome, says that God, true to His covenant with Abraham, brought the Messiah into the world through Jews and within the Jewish community. But Judaism as an institution would not accept the Messiah. They were like an olive tree whose natural branches had been broken off and wild branches had to be grafted in. But why?

Romans 11:20 tells us it was simply due to their unbelief. The root remained a Jewish root, but the subsequent branches for over 2,000 years have been primarily Gentile branches, and Paul says in Romans 11:25 that this hardening on the part of Israel will continue until the fullness of the Gentiles has come in.

That is one reason why we would expect the first believers to be Jews. However, there is another side of this which should raise questions in our minds. According to 2 Peter 3:9, part of the nature of God is that He is, *"... not wanting anyone to perish, but everyone to come to repentance."* For God there is neither Jew nor Gentile, slave nor free, male nor female (Galatians 3:28). The clear intentions of Jesus Himself were that the gospel should spread among the Gentiles as well as the Jews. When He was about to depart, the commission He left His disciples was clearly to make disciples of <u>all</u> nations.

The Greek word Jesus used for nations was *ethne*, which today we call peoples or people groups. Jesus of course knew this. He was very aware that He was the Son of God - the long-awaited Messiah. He knew that when He died on the cross, the blood He shed would be for the remission of sins for everyone, both Jew and Gentile.

He knew that He was now beginning a process of redemption which would eventually culminate with that great multitude in heaven comprising all nations, all tribes, peoples and tongues, standing before the throne of the Lamb (Revelation 7:9).

So, the question persists, why were the one and twenty disciples who surrounded Jesus at the beginning of the book of Acts all Jews? Why stick to the Jews when He knew it was the Father's plan to bring salvation to everyone?

Jesus made it clear that He had come to bring salvation to all mankind - the kingdom of God was for Jews and non-Jews. So, if His reasons for maintaining a Jewish group had little to do with theology, perhaps they were for reasons of methodology.

Assuming that Jesus had planned a systematic strategy for His three short years of ministry, as opposed to just letting it all happen randomly, could it be possible that He intended to set a pattern for the future of all Christian missions? If so, Jesus might have been modelling an important principle that plays a key role in contemporary missions. A principle that a number of mission specialists have referred to as the 'people approach' to world evangelisation. As church growth specialist Donald McGavran once said: *"People prefer to become Christians without crossing racial, linguistic or class barriers."*

Culture is something that most people do not take lightly, as those who study mankind are quick to inform us. Even though the gospel of Jesus Christ transcends all cultures, it is still true that violating, denigrating or challenging the way of life or the way of thinking of a particular people group has proven to be a very poor way of subsequently attracting them to the Gospel.

Although there may be some variations and exceptions, modern missiology teaches that the most viable strategy for extending the Kingdom of God through the world, is to set targets, people group by people group. What is a people group? The Lausanne Committee for World Evangelisation arrived at this definition many years ago:

A people group is a significantly large sociological grouping of individuals who perceive themselves to have a common affinity for one another. From the viewpoint of evangelism, this is the largest possible group within which the gospel can spread without encountering barriers of understanding or acceptance.

The Jews were one such people group in Jesus' day, but within this group there was a considerable variety - from Matthew, a tax collector working for the Roman government through to Simon the Zealot who was totally committed to overthrowing the same government! Yet in spite of the differences in politics, age and personality, they belonged to the same ethnic group. They had the same colour skin; they shared similar cultural values, which including prejudices; they all ate and abstained from eating the same foods; spoke the same language and perceived themselves to have a common affinity for one another. If the people group approach to bringing the world to Christ is based on this high view of individual cultures, how can we justify that Biblically?

Culture is often seen as a barrier that encourages separation and social disharmony. Some think of cultural differences as an evil which needs to be ignored, if not stamped out. Their goal is to assimilate all peoples into one language and one culture. In the world today, however, such a goal is being seriously challenged theologically by some mission scholars, and from a practical, sociological point of view, such a goal is totally unrealistic.

My nation of Australia, for example, is now famously one of the most multi-cultural nations in the whole world. Despite the best efforts of some isolated political voices, we are beginning to accept, appreciate and even celebrate our cultural diversity and recognise the integrity of each and every people group.

As Christians, we need to get back to the Bible and understand that God is the creator of human cultures, and we need to accept that God had something to do with the makeup of our society. There are three important insights which can help us understand multi-culturalism in a positive light.

1. The human race is one.

All the diverse people groups on the earth ultimately belong to one family. God created Adam and Eve to be the forbears of all humankind. If we go back far enough, we will find that every human being is genetically related to every other human being.

Paul affirms this in his sermon in Athens in Acts 17:26 when he said: *"From one man God made every nation of men, that they should inhabit the whole earth; and he determined the times set for them and the exact places where they should live."*

This is the basis for the Biblical truth that in the community of the Kingdom of God there is no difference before God between Jews and Gentiles.

2. God intended humans to be one, but diverse.

Although it is true that the Kingdom of God welcomes Jews and Gentiles on an equal basis, it is also true that in this present life each culture is distinct. As we look at the Biblical evidence, we discover that this distinction and the uniqueness of all people groups is part of God's creative design. Biologically speaking, the genes and chromosomes of Adam & Eve had to contain all the genetic material for the human diversity we see today. The first Biblical list of human people groups appears as far back as Genesis chapter 10 - called by some as 'The Table of the Nations.'

According to Genesis 10:5, each people group was separated into their lands, each according to their own language and family. The way that came about is recorded in Genesis 11 in that well known story of the Tower of Babel, when God decided in one action to confuse their language so they may not understand each other (Genesis 11:7).

Now the most common interpretation I have heard of the Tower of Babel story is that this was God's punishment for the sinful rebellion of mankind and that the result was disorder across the international world - it was not the plan and purpose of God. This interpretation is very common and is often used by those advocating for racial reconciliation and integration.

However, I believe this negative interpretation is not compatible with a Christian understanding of cultures. It's also inconsistent with contemporary views concerning world mission. Suggesting that the diversity of our human cultures only has its root in human sin, rather than in the purposes of God, is not the only way to understand Genesis 10 & 11. It is my belief that the sinful rebellion at the tower of Babel was actually an effort on the part of humanity to prevent us from becoming diversified, according to God's plan.

From the very beginning, God had set in motion His design to separate humans into people groups so they could *"Be fruitful and multiply and fill the earth"* as He said to Adam. However, the early human race, who still all spoke one language, rebelled against this plan of God. They intuitively perceived that as they multiplied, families and clusters of families would need more land for farming and hunting and that if they continued to scatter across the earth - their social separation would then produce increasing differences in their culture.

The reason they started to build the tower and the city around it, is clearly stated in Genesis 11:4: so that they would *"... not be scattered over the face of the whole earth."* Their supreme fear was to allow God to diversify them, and they were willing to make a pact with the devil himself, if necessary, in order to prevent it. We all know that scheme didn't work because God sovereignly intervened to achieve His purposes. God accomplished in an instant what ordinarily would have taken centuries to achieve. He changed a mono-lingual society into a multi-lingual society. This effectively stopped them building the tower and the city and rapidly accelerated the geographical scattering of the people groups - each now with its own language.

A growing number of Biblical scholars have now abandoned the traditional, negative interpretation of the Tower of Babel story and have begun to see that diversity is neither a condemnation nor a punishment. Ethnic pluralism, or multiculturalism is to be welcomed as a divine blessing, not resisted as a curse. This high view of human culture and its origins is a very valuable building block for formulating any sound, biblical and practical strategy for reaching the world for Jesus Christ.

3. God is concerned to bring all peoples to Himself.

In 1 Timothy 6:15, Paul speaks of Jesus Christ as, *"the only Ruler, the King of kings and Lord of lords."* In Matthew 24:14 we read that *" .. this gospel of the kingdom will be preached in the whole world as a testimony to all nations ..."*

The way God's master plan has been and is being implemented most effectively in the world today is through the people group approach to world evangelisation. In order to sort out the most appropriate evangelistic methods of spreading the gospel to all the people groups in the world, it is helpful for us to understand the various kinds of evangelism which exist.

Basically, there are three levels of evangelism that apply in our multicultural world. The experts have come up with some very creative labels - they call them E1, E2 and E3.

E1 is that first stage of evangelisation in which the only barrier we have to cross if we have a burden for the lost and desire to bring them to Jesus, is what they call the stained-glass barrier. That is, we need to get out of the church building and into the community around us. This is a barrier for many of us who have settled down quite nicely into our protective Christian ghetto.

This is actually the easiest level of evangelism because in most cases, the people outside the church building are of the same culture - they speak the same language. They are people with whom we can more easily identify from a cultural and human perspective, as we bring them the gospel.

Now E2 and E3 are the areas of evangelism where we must cross a cultural barrier of some kind in order to present the truth of Jesus Christ to the lost. The basic difference between E2 and E3 is the degree to which that cultural barrier exists. E2 is the level where we cross the first barrier and get out of the church fortress and into the society around us, but then encounter another barrier as we discover a culture within a culture. Increasingly, this is what we are facing in Australia as our cultural diversity continues to intensify and grow.

For example, if we desire to bring the gospel to the Aboriginal people around us or to the Chinese or Indian people in our region, we will need to cross this extra cultural barrier. This is E2 evangelism because we have two barriers to cross. There's the cultural barrier between the church and the unchurched, and then the barrier of a different culture within our culture.

These people are still part of our society, they are still part of our culture by virtue of the fact they live amongst us, and this makes it a little easier, yet we need to respect that they are also part of a culture which may be radically different to our native culture. These different people groups are not just ethnic groups. The largest people group within most cities that is part of our culture and language and yet have a totally different set of priorities and ways of dealing with life, is the youth.

People under 25 in this culture can no longer be reached through E1 evangelism. There is a greater difference than at any point in the past. There was a time when youth leaders and youth pastors could be 30 or 40 years of age and still relate well to young people. This is clearly the exception now in Australia. The most effective ministry to youth today is taking place where leaders are themselves under 25 years of age.

The church is slowly beginning to understand and accept that if we keep complaining about how rebellious and different today's youth are and don't find ways to cross the cultural barrier and speak to them in their language, relating the truth of the Gospel through their cultural mindset, then we may not have a church in our community in another generation.

The third level of Evangelism, E3, is when we take the gospel into another culture in their own setting. This is what we have traditionally called missions, where we go to another people group in their native land. Socially and culturally, they are really totally separate to us. This is surely the most challenging form of evangelism.

Now we need to understand that this separation is cultural and social; spiritual and lingual, but sometimes it is not geographical. More and more in this nation and others, we are discovering whole cultures which exist largely untouched by the culture around them. So, as you've heard it said many times, you don't need to leave your country to become a missionary. There is now more truth in that statement than in any previous generation.

Most people are won to Christ through E1 evangelism, whereby churches in local communities are reaching out within their own culture. Most evangelists are mono-cultural evangelists. Most Pastors are mono-cultural Pastors. It has always been this way and will remain that way until Jesus returns because God calls and equips most people to minister primarily to those people in their own culture - but not all. God has also called some people to use their particular spiritual gifts in very different cultures. If He hadn't, then Christianity would never have spread across the world like it has. Those whom God has called to minister in those second two levels of evangelism He has also equipped with a missionary gifting.

Given the fact that thousands of unreached people groups have yet to be brought the gospel, it may come as a surprise to learn that less than 1% of committed Christians appear to have been given that missionary gift. Low as that might sound, the fact is that less than half this number of Christians around the world are actively engaged in cross cultural ministries.

In fact, if as many as 1% of the world-wide church was ever mobilised, then the resulting missionary force would be more than adequate to reach all unreached people groups in this present generation. 1% is a far more significant number that it first appears!

How can it be done with so few? It's really simple and it goes back to the fact that most evangelism is mono-cultural (E1). The job for cross-cultural ministers is to plant the gospel in a people group by E2 and E3 evangelism methods, but then to equip the leaders of that culture to carry on E1 level of evangelism.

If you have had anything at all to do with overseas missions or have read magazines which tell us about cross-cultural ministry, you will have read or heard that nationals evangelise far better than missionaries. E1 evangelism is by far the most effective. Kooris preaching to Kooris; Chinese preaching to Chinese; youth preaching to youth; elderly to elderly; even men to men and women to women. That then brings us right back to our original question in the book of Acts: Why is it that Jesus' nucleus of one hundred and twenty believers were all Jews? The answer is because Jesus, like 99% of Christians that followed Him, was a mono-cultural minister.

I am speaking here of Jesus' human ministry. His three years as an iterant preacher. In that role, God had called and equipped Him to be an E1 evangelist. Even Jesus operated within the reality of humanity when it came to evangelism and most of us can relate to His E1 style of evangelism where He ministered primarily within one people group. That's why I said earlier that I believe Jesus' three years of single-culture ministry to the Jews was a strategic choice, not a theological position.

As far as we know from the Bible, Jesus did not train any of His disciples for cross-cultural ministry, although some may have ended up there later. So, the first genuine E3 ministry appearing in the book of Acts would be in chapter 8 where we read of Philip preaching to the Samaritans. Some more radical E3 cross-cultural missionaries would be those who went from Cyprus to Cyrene to the Gentiles in Antioch in chapter 11. And of course, the most outstanding example would be the Apostle Paul who became known as the Apostle to the Gentiles. All of this missiology theory is really important to know and to understand, especially in our nation of Australia, if we are to effectively bring the gospel of Jesus Christ to a needy world.

The mission field is on our doorstep. There was a time not too long ago when most of us could be totally oblivious to E2 and E3 level evangelism - unless we were gifted and called as overseas missionaries; a time when the vast majority of Christians only had to cross that first barrier … the stained-glass barrier … and enter a familiar culture. Today, however, we have hundreds of fully developed and distinctly different cultures living together in this great melting pot we call Australia.

In the next chapter we will look in more detail at Jesus' methods of evangelism and I hope and pray that the Holy Spirit will give us some practical handles to grab on to in order to bring the grace and mercy of God into the lives of people in our community and across our nation.

CHAPTER THREE
Ready for the Ride?

This book will be focussing on the book of Acts, but before I get into the actual text, I have taken the first two chapters to address some important 'big picture' realities. I provided some valuable background information concerning the book of Acts and in particular, the multicultural aspects of the society which existed at the time.

They were more lectures in Missiology than chapters to inspire, but I believe they will become increasingly valuable as we explore the book of Acts in more detail.

It is really important that we don't have our brains in neutral when studying the Bible. It's too easy to spiritualise everything and miss the big picture. There is no doubt that the Bible was inspired by God and that reading it without the supernatural anointing of the Spirit will rob us of its power and relevance.

However, it is also valid and important for us to look at things like context and the make-up of societies both then and now. Sociology has replaced faith for many and that is sad, but that does not make sociology evil or inappropriate in itself. It can be very valuable.

I affirm again that it is Jesus Christ Who builds His church, but how does He do that? He builds His church in partnership with people like you and me and so we need to clearly understand the complex structure of human society in order to identify the doors that God may open. We need to have the cultural sensitivity to participate in His ministry rather than work against it through our ignorance.

There is much we can learn from those mission specialists who have gone to hundreds of countries around the world to research, observe and report on what God is doing in the task of world evangelisation and what we can do or not do to participate in that vital ministry.

Now let me reiterate that the catchy and somewhat provocative title of this book was not chosen in haste. The 'giant' to which I refer is the church of Jesus Christ.

The church is a giant because she is the Bride of Christ; the church is a giant because she was created and is sustained and empowered by none other than the Spirit of God Himself: the church is a giant because she embodies the manifest presence of the King; the church is a giant because she is the most influential and relevant organisation on the face of the earth; the church is a giant because she is the sole custodian of the solutions to all of this world's problems. I could go on for some time, but I think even this brief resume would allow me the freedom to call the church a giant.

So why the *sleeping* giant? I think you already know. When we look at the church through God's eyes and through the eyes of the New Testament - she is most definitely a giant. But when we look at the visible church today through the eyes of a lost and needy society - particularly in our city and our nation - this giant is, for all intents and purposes – asleep on the job!

The church has very little real impact on the world around it anymore. In the eternal Kingdom of God, the church is all those things I said and more, but in the human kingdom of this world, we Christians need to wake up and get in touch with our roots and the reality of who we are in Christ so the world can see the reality, the power and the impact of the church.

I am not implying for one moment that the church which Jesus promised to build will cannot be built without us and will not be perfect in every respect. That is an established fact. What this this book will attempt to do, as clearly portrayed in the title, is wake us up to acknowledge and step into the practical outworking of the true church.

We need to become in practice who we already are in theory. We need to wake up and be mobilised to let the truth of who we are in the eternal Kingdom of God shine into the darkness of the kingdom of this world.

I know who we are in Christ. I know how precious and perfect and spotless and powerful the church is in the eternal Kingdom of God - hallelujah for that - but brothers and sisters, until the glory and purity and beauty and relevance and power of the church of Jesus Christ impacts the darkness and despair and sickness and need of this society - that church is sound asleep and ineffective in this world! While we all sleep and enjoy life in the comfort and protection of our Christian fortresses, there are thousands of people surrounding us every single day who are not going to know about Jesus until the next life, even though the Lord commissioned you and me to tell them now!

So, if you don't think the church needs waking up in this city and this nation then stick around and journey through the book of Acts with me and you may change your mind. If, after going through the book of Acts, you still don't think the giant is asleep today, then perhaps you're not asleep - you may be in a coma!

This leads me to an important point about life in God's Kingdom. When Jesus said that we are <u>in</u> this world but not <u>of</u> this world, He was trying to explain the reality of the two kingdoms in which Christians find themselves. Until we really understand this, and embrace this reality, we will struggle with a lot of teaching about our position in Christ.

For example: Do you believe that you are holy in the sight of God because of the finished work of Christ? If you believe that God has given you the righteousness and holiness of Christ as a free gift in salvation - hallelujah - because that is the truth!

> *"For if, by the trespass of the one man, death reigned through that one man, how much more will those who receive God's abundant provision of grace and of the gift of righteousness reign in life through the one man, Jesus Christ!" (Romans 5:17)*

> *"But now he has reconciled you by Christ's physical body through death to present you holy in his sight, without blemish and free from accusation ..." (Colossians 1:22)*

Therefore, in the sight of God; before all of heaven; in the eternal Kingdom of God; you and I are spotless, clean, righteous, holy and perfect because the righteousness of Christ has been given to us as a gift. So, let me ask you something, have you committed any sins at all in the last month? Have you been 100% obedient to every command of God and have not strayed at all? I am pretty sure I know the answers.

We are exhorted in Scripture to be holy - to flee from sin and evil. We are exhorted to make the right choices so that our life in this world will match up with our life in Christ. So, you see our holiness in the sight of God is not negotiable. If we believe on the Lord Jesus Christ, we shall embrace our salvation, we shall take our place as part of the spotless Bride of Christ – the church. But we all continue in this fallen flesh in a world run by the powers of darkness - powers that continue to tempt, entice and attack us. We therefore need to make some clear choices if our life in the Kingdom of God is going to be seen and make a difference in this broken and needy world.

When Jesus suggested we pray: *"Your Kingdom come, Your will be done, on earth as it is in heaven ..."* He gave us the only key to understanding everything in this fallen world. When Jesus came, He brought the reality of heaven to earth. He released; He ushered in; He birthed the Kingdom of God among us and brought men, women and young people into that Kingdom as they trusted in Him. He came as a divine conqueror for one purpose - so that the Kingdom of God would come face to face with the kingdom of Satan. The coming of Jesus was therefore a declaration of war against the powers of darkness and we can see that war unfold on every page of the book of Acts.

Since that time the kingdom of God has been slowly, but forcefully eclipsing the kingdom of this world. As new covenant, redeemed children of God, we are now right in the middle of that action. Every day we face the reality of sin, suffering, hate and pain. Every day we face our own shortcomings, rebellion and pride. Every day we see the reality of this fallen world and that's the only world the majority of people around us will ever see.

However, you and I, and all Christians know a very different reality because we are also citizens of another Kingdom. We may be seeing the darkness and despair of this world every day, but we are connected to the light and life and power of heaven. It's that conflict; it's that cosmic battle which defines our whole existence and provides us with a reason for even being here.

So, you see, in the Kingdom of God, we are already righteous, pure, holy, redeemed and purchased by the blood of the Lamb. But in this human realm, we face the same sin and failure and dirt we always have. Therefore, if the holiness, righteousness and purity that is within us is ever going to be seen by the world, we need to make some daily choices about our attitude and actions as we deal ruthlessly with sin when it rears its ugly head - not to please God or to earn His forgiveness and mercy - but to allow the life of Christ within us to emerge so that world will see Jesus and embrace His salvation.

Another key example of living in two kingdoms is in the area of forgiveness. Understanding our dual citizenship will overcome the conflicts in dealing with passages on forgiveness. The Bible makes it very clear that we are forgiven, once and for all time, through the life, death and resurrection of Jesus. In the eyes of God, in the eternal Kingdom of God, our sins are forgiven - past, present and future - whether we confess them or not, whether we ask for forgiveness or not. The slate is wiped totally clean in the eyes of God and that was achieved by Jesus.

However, in this world, in this kingdom where Satan continues to reign; we need to deal ruthlessly with sin and ensure that we confess it and appropriate or apply and walk in the forgiveness of God every day. Otherwise, Satan will inhabit our sin and bring hell into our lives. That is why you should make sure there is no unforgiveness in your heart. Unforgiveness, resentment and bitterness are like red carpet rolled out to the powers of darkness for them to march in and destroy your life. You will still make it to heaven because Jesus secured a place for you 2,000 years ago, but with unforgiveness in your heart, you're going to get a taste of hell along the way in this earthly kingdom!

I suggest that unless we understand who we are in Christ and know, beyond any doubt, our eternal security in Him and our permanent resident status in the Kingdom of Heaven, we will struggle along the road of life, plagued by guilt and shame and left never really knowing who we are or what we are to do.

We must understand that we still carry around our fallen flesh through which Satan can inflict his ministry of discouragement, dissension, division and death - and our sin, our unforgiveness and unholy actions invite his ministry and bring the full force of darkness down upon us and others around us.

So, let me affirm once more that you and I and all who profess faith in the Lord Jesus Christ are part of the precious, perfect, pure, spotless Bride - the church of Jesus Christ. But I also affirm that in this life, while ever the Lord leaves us here in this world which is dominated by evil, it is our responsibility to make the right choices every day that will align our thoughts, our prayers, our priorities, our activities, our efforts, our hard work to the truth of who we really are in Christ.

We face choices every day: we can act in a way that is consistent with who we are as the church of Jesus Christ, or we can act in a way that is inconsistent with our true identity. That is why I am bold enough to refer to the church as a sleeping giant.

That is why we are looking at the book of Acts, because here we are reminded that it is Jesus Christ who builds His church; we are reminded of who we really are in Christ; we are reminded that the power that dwells within us and every disciple is the same power which created the whole universe and raised Jesus from the dead; we are reminded that all of this is made possible by God and not by us.

However, we really need to understand that it's equally true that if we choose to not participate in what God is doing; if we do not align our choices and our prayers and our whole lives with what God has already achieved in Christ, then in this life we will not see the church wake up.

Others will - many are experiencing the power of that giant right now as she sweeps across whole villages, cities and nations - but we will never see that in our nation if the church remains an activity on our daily planner - rather than the life we live and our true identity!

Until we reconnect with the power, the glory, the reality and the priority of the church which Jesus established and promised to build, Christians across this great nation will continue to be an irrelevant minority group which has no impact on our society.

There are certainly some nonrepeatable events in Acts, there are also some transitional happenings; but the many basic spiritual principles are the same today as when Peter and Paul ministered. In our study of this important book, we need to look beyond the accidentals to the essentials and discover afresh the spiritual dynamics of the Word of God and prayer, love and fellowship, persecution and personal witness for Jesus Christ.

I wish I could tell you how much you are going to enjoy this book - but I can't. Because you won't enjoy it at all if you actually take it seriously. If you look in mirror of God's Word and see what it says to you, for a while it will be anything but enjoyable! We will not be able to truly examine the book of Acts without having our whole life and every principle and priority we have, challenged head-on by the Spirit of God.

However, if we choose to face that challenge with determination, courage and the willingness to let the Spirit of God transform us, the result will be a fruitful, active, powerful, nation-transforming church as God intended and the joy that will flood our hearts will remove any memory of the struggle we had getting there.

None of us enjoy a trip to the dentist, but after it's over and the pain and memory fade, the result is amazing! So, this will not be a hand-stroking, back-patting book that makes us all feel like we've made it. Nor will it forget the truth that our salvation and our security in Christ has nothing at all to do with our personal performance.

That truth will remain in my preaching and writing as long as I draw breath. However, in case you hadn't noticed, the world in which you and I live is in a real mess and it will not get better without a major intervention from the only One Who can fix it.

Jesus is the way, the truth and the life. Jesus is the only answer to every spiritual, political, social, psychological and physical problem in the world. But unless His Body; unless those who are indwelt by His very life and power don't decide to get off their backsides and get reconnected with the urgency and the priority of His mission in this world, the church will remain peripheral to the world around us, which is never what God intended.

Brother or sister in Christ, please understand what I am saying here. We are not going to move this world by criticism or by conformity, but by the combustion within it of lives ignited by the Spirit of God. The early church had none of the things that we think are so essential for success today – buildings, money, political influence, social status - and yet that church won multitudes to Christ and saw many congregations established throughout the Roman-controlled world. Why? Because the church had the power of the Spirit energizing her ministry. The church comprised people who were ignited by the Holy Spirit.

The same Holy Spirit is available to us today to make us more effective witnesses for Jesus Christ. The ministry of the Spirit is to glorify Christ in the life and witness of the believer (John 16:14) and that is what is important. God's people today share the same dynamic that energized the early believers. If we are yielded to the Spirit, we can be adding new chapters to the exciting story of the church every day! That is God's plan. That is our purpose.

None of that will happen if the giant remains asleep.

CHAPTER FOUR
An Important Prayer Meeting

As we finally start to wrestle with the text in the book of Acts, I want to stress that I will not be doing a verse-by-verse analysis and many of the verses won't even be referenced in the sermons. This book will be long enough with me focussing on the main themes and theological principles, it would require many books if I went verse by verse! However, I want to really encourage you to make sure you read all the text as we go through and for this chapter, that would mean the first chapter of Acts.

If I gave the book of Acts to a Hollywood writer and asked them to prepare the script for a movie, I am pretty sure that movie would not begin in Acts 1. Like every good James Bond movie, they would want this story to begin with a dynamic action scene which immediately captures the attention of everyone, drawing them to the edge of their seats – as they are caught up in the drama of the opening scene.

That would probably mean they would start with the coming of the Holy Spirit on the Day of Pentecost in chapter 2. In fact, a lot of scholars over the years have wondered why Luke didn't start his second work with that dynamic story.

The fact is, the early disciples could never have become dynamic instruments for the extension of God's Kingdom if they had not obeyed the command of Jesus to wait for the promise Jesus gave them before leaving the earth to return to the Father's side.

> "I am going to send you what my Father has promised; but stay in the city until you have been clothed with power from on high." (Luke 24:49)

It is worth noting that this waiting took ten days - no longer. In our Christian life there must be a balance between spending time with God in worship, praise, intimacy and waiting on Him, and in fulfilling the ministry of Jesus in ministry and outreach.

The Upper Room, where the Disciples spent a good part of these ten days, appears to be a place of peace and quiet and security. There is little doubt that the Holy Spirit was present there in an unusual way. I can just imagine that much time would have been spent looking back and thanking God for Jesus, for all that His life and ministry had meant to these followers.

Times such as these in warm fellowship with other believers in the presence of God are precious. Through prayer, we are drawn into a close and fulfilling relationship with God. We can imagine that in the Upper Room the Disciples were probably discovering who they were in Christ. Undoubtedly, time would have been spent in worship and praise, pouring out their soul to God.

It would have been a special time where God received them as they were, rather than evaluating them for what they did or didn't do. It must have seemed to them like a foretaste of heaven, where one day we will all be around God's throne, exalting Him and worshipping His name.

All that for ten days. But as we see later, suddenly the *"until"* took effect, and they received the power for which they had all been waiting. From then on, it was action, ministry and the practical outworking of the power they had received. Within 24 hours they had welcomed 3,000 unpolished disciples of Christ into the family, all of whom needed discipleship, nurture and care in their new Christian journey. The action sparked that day actually continued for the thirty-year time-span of the book of Acts, with notable pauses, such as the Apostles' desire to give themselves continually to prayer and the ministry of the Word as we read in chapter 6.

Now, nothing is particularly significant about the period of ten days. The Apostle Paul, who had not been with Jesus personally, needed several years for his waiting time before God launched him into active ministry. The point is this, time for pre-ministry formation is critically important, but we must not allow that time to continue indefinitely. There's important work to be done!

My concern is that we do not fall into a rut and become what some refer to as professional tarriers. Of course, waiting is not optional - it is necessary. If we do not have the intimacy with God, we will not have the power or the direction.

Waiting on God is essential. It is as necessary as food is to the human body. However, like food, waiting can be overdone. Physical obesity can prevent our bodies from being all that God intends them to be. Spiritual obesity can have similar outcomes. If we do not ever get out of the Upper Room and into the marketplace, we will probably never be part of the mission and ministry of Jesus in the world today.

> *"For John baptized with water, but in a few days, you will be baptized with the Holy Spirit." Then they gathered around him and asked him, "Lord, are you at this time going to restore the kingdom to Israel?" He said to them: "It is not for you to know the times or dates the Father has set by his own authority. But you will receive power when the Holy Spirit comes on you; and you will be my witnesses in Jerusalem, and in all Judea and Samaria, and to the ends of the earth." (Acts 1:5-8)*

Their question must have filled Jesus with dismay. Were they still so lacking in perception? The verb 'restore' shows that they were expecting a political and territorial kingdom. The noun 'Israel' shows that they were expecting a national kingdom. The adverbial clause 'at this time' shows that they were expecting its immediate establishment.

Tragically, many people today seem to embrace similar concepts about the Kingdom of God. Of course, it is our Christian duty to strive for justice and righteousness and freedom and prosperity in our society. But some carry this too far and seem to forget the words of Paul in 2 Corinthians 10:4 where he reminds us that our weapons in this spiritual battle are not of this world.

So, as we have seen many times over the years, people begin to walk according to the flesh by using force and political coercion and man's methods to accomplish what they believe to be God's Kingdom values.

But the book of Acts clearly shows us that the crucial force for ushering in the Kingdom of God across the whole earth is the power of the Holy Spirit and personal witness.

> *"For John baptized with water, but in a few days, you will be baptized with the Holy Spirit." (Acts 1:5)*

Spiritual power for advancing the Kingdom of God would come through the baptism of the Holy Spirit. Unfortunately, many differences in interpretation of what the baptism of the Holy Spirit means have been used by Satan to divide segments of the Body of Christ for over a hundred years now. However, a brief look at some of the terms may just help to cool the fires of the debate and help us get past the conflict that has arisen.

DSifferent terms are used for the power-bestowing experience which Luke is describing here. *'Baptism of the Holy Spirit'* is one term; *'The Holy Spirit has come upon you'* is another. Then the verb *'filled'* in reference to the Holy Spirit, is used four other times in the book of Acts.

It is used a second time for Peter who was filled with the Holy Spirit (4:8); in Acts 4:31 the believers were again filled with the Holy Spirit when they assembled for a prayer meeting; In Acts 9:11, Ananias ministered to Saul in Damascus to be filled with the Holy Spirit and in Acts 13:9 Paul was again filled with the Holy Spirit for his power-encounter with the sorcerer.

The expression, *'filled with the Holy Spirit'* is used only once in the Epistles (Ephesians 5:18) where Paul is contrasting it with being drunk (filled) with wine. Paul uses *'baptised in the Holy Spirit'* only once in his letters in 1 Corinthians 12:13 where he says that we were all baptised into one body by one Spirit.

Issues such as whether we are 'baptised' or 'filled' with the Holy Spirit once or many times; whether it occurs at conversion or subsequent to conversion; or whether there is some initial physical evidence to certify that it has happened - are more important to some Christian leaders today than others.

In spite of the divisions and debates surrounding these issues, the reason they are raised in the first place is valid and that is because we all need the supernatural power of the Holy Spirit in our lives and in our ministries to the greatest extent possible in order to fulfill the mission of Christ in the world.

I hope and pray that the divisive debates about how this happens will soon be a thing of past. I long for the day when every sincere believer will be more concerned about having the ministry of the Holy Spirit in their lives than about how and when it happens.

> *"But you will receive power when the Holy Spirit comes on you; and you will be my witnesses in Jerusalem, and in all Judea and Samaria, and to the ends of the earth." (Acts 1:8)*

In this verse we have what effectively is the fifth appearance of the Great Commission of Jesus in the New Testament. Those five passages are: Matthew 28:16-20; Mark 16:14-18; Luke 24:44-49; John 20:19-23; and Acts 1:4-8. Four of them (John being the exception) specify the global scope of the evangelistic task given by Jesus. On another occasion Jesus said,

> *"… this gospel of the kingdom will be preached in the whole world as a testimony to all nations, and then the end will come." (Matthew 24:14)*

This seems to indicate that world evangelisation is not an endless task, but that it's following a divine timeline. The specific plan is to plant Christian churches in every nation (or within every people group).

Missions experts are now suggesting that there appears to be light at the end of the Great Commission tunnel. For the first time in history there is good reason to believe that the church of Jesus Christ, as represented on earth today, has sufficient resources to complete the task of preaching the gospel of Jesus Christ to every people group, within this current generation.

Missiologist, George Otis Jnr, had this to say back at the end of the twentieth century:

"The soldiers of the Lord of Hosts have now circled the final strongholds of the serpent - namely the nations and spiritual principalities contained within the 10/40 window. While the remaining task is admittedly the most challenging phase of the battle, the armies of Satan are now faced with a large community of believers whose spiritual resources, if properly motivated, submitted and unified are truly awesome. If the forces of God continue to push back the powers of darkness at the current rate, then before most of us alive today leave this earth, we will see the day when a baby born anywhere in the world will have the same chance to hear the good news of Jesus Christ."

When I speak about the end of the 'Great Commission tunnel' I am not saying that everyone in the world will embrace Jesus as their Saviour, rather that everybody will be within reasonable reach of the Gospel. In other words, this gospel of the Kingdom will have been preached to all the world as a witness to all the nations, just as Jesus said.

Now, obviously, no human plan or strategies could ever possibly accomplish this task before this current generation leaves the earth. It can only be done through an extraordinary outpouring of supernatural power through the Holy Spirit. Is that likely?

Well, who would have thought that the Iron Curtain would be torn down so fast? Who would have predicted the demise of communism in eastern Europe? Who would have thought that whole nations would go from being 2% Christian to over 60% Christian in less than 50 years? Things have occurred in the past fifty years which previous generations would never have even dreamed of. The expectation and anticipation of an outpouring of God's Spirit is growing by the day.

Of course, the final thrust will undoubtedly involve the most challenging battle since the powers of darkness took mankind captive in the garden of Eden. No sensible missiologist is predicting dates or times, there's no clear prophetic insight that the Lord will return soon. No one knows the hour nor the day, but one thing is certain, we are closer than we have even been.

"After he said this, he was taken up before their very eyes, and a cloud hid him from their sight."(Acts 1:9)

This event, which we call the ascension, marked the end of the earthly ministry of Jesus. He will not appear in person again until His second coming. During His life on earth, and particularly towards the end, Jesus tried to prepare His disciples for His imminent departure. They loved Him so much that it was not easy for them to accept the fact that He would leave them alone. Peter was so upset at one point that he almost rebuked Jesus when He dared suggest that He would die soon. Jesus sharply reprimanded him.

Later, Jesus calmly explained to them that it was to their advantage that He leave them (John 16:7). But how could this be, they thought? How could anything be an advantage over being with Jesus personally?

Quite simply Jesus told them that only if He went away could He send the Holy Spirit, Who would be with them in a way that He could never be in the flesh. It would be to their advantage to have the Holy Spirit Who was not tied to one place and time like Jesus was as a man. When they were indwelt by the Holy Spirit they would have access to the only power that would overcome the enemy who had kept men and women in bondage for centuries.

To even begin to fulfill the Great Commission, they needed a power that was equal to the power that created the universe and raised Jesus from the dead. That power would only be available to them if Jesus returned to heaven and sent the Comforter, the Counsellor, the Spirit of grace, the Holy Spirit of God.

It would be through the indwelling and all-consuming power of the Holy Spirit that the disciples would be able to see the fruit of Jesus' promise that they would do what He had done and even greater than that! For the most part, the disciples were ready for Jesus' departure, and by then they thought they understood.

Even so, they were bewildered when He actually ascended into heaven before their eyes. They stared into the clouds so long that two angels had to come and move them along!

> *"They were looking intently up into the sky as he was going, when suddenly two men dressed in white stood beside them. "Men of Galilee," they said, "why do you stand here looking into the sky? This same Jesus, who has been taken from you into heaven, will come back in the same way you have seen him go into heaven." (Acts 1:10-11)*

This brought the disciples back to their senses and they went to Jerusalem and joined what was history's most powerful prayer meeting.

> *"Then the apostles returned to Jerusalem from the hill called the Mount of Olives, a Sabbath day's walk from the city. When they arrived, they went upstairs to the room where they were staying. Those present were Peter, John, James and Andrew; Philip and Thomas, Bartholomew and Matthew; James, son of Alphaeus and Simon the Zealot, and Judas son of James. They all joined together constantly in prayer, along with the women and Mary the mother of Jesus, and with his brothers. In those days Peter stood up among the believers (a group numbering about a hundred and twenty)." (Acts 1:12-15)*

In his Gospel, Luke also says these disciples continued in praise and worship. The combination of praise, worship, sincere prayer and supplication is an unbeatable formula for drawing near to God, opening ourselves to the voice of the Spirit and learning what the Father is doing. Ten days in prayer is a very long prayer meeting. I think most of us would have a hard time trying to block out ten whole days for worship and prayer.

However, as we look around the world today, more than at any point in the church's history, men, women and young people are beginning to give this kind of priority to prayer and worship. Three-day and four-day prayer summits are happening across the world and growing in popularity.

Pastors, leaders and intercessors are beginning to see that it is possible to spend that kind of time in prayer and worship. Once you get over the initial hurdle and allow the Lord to lead - the time flies. These first disciples were re-grouping to begin the process of world evangelisation and they knew from the outset that the task before them required extraordinary spiritual power.

There is no indication they knew the prayer meeting would last for ten days. They only knew that it was *"not many days from now."* So, they settled in for the long haul and seemed prepared to pray until they knew beyond any shadow of doubt that God had responded.

Would God have responded if they had decided to take a well-earned rest? You could hardly blame them after all they had been through if they wanted to lie on the beach at Joppa for a few days. This is not a superficial question, because it raises the whole issue of whether prayer has any effect on God's actions.

I realise that many people who hold a very high view of God's sovereignty would assert that our prayer doesn't change God, it only changes us, and there's some truth in that statement. God is eternal and unchangeable and His character and nature are not altered by anything that occurs in His creation, but there is no doubt that this ten-day prayer meeting would have brought deep and significant changes in the disciples themselves. And yet our sovereign God has indicated that our actions are not inconsequential:

> *"Call to me and I will answer you and tell you great and unsearchable things you do not know." (Jeremiah 33:3)*

> *"If my people, who are called by my name, will humble themselves and pray and seek my face and turn from their wicked ways, then will I hear from heaven and will forgive their sin and will heal their land." (2 Chronicles 7:14)*

The whole world has now been blessed because the disciples decided to be obedient to the Lord and give themselves to prayer for ten days.

Not only were the disciples consistent and obedient, but they were also unified. They continued 'with one accord.' One reason corporate prayer is often more effective than individual prayer is because of the principle of agreement.

> *"...truly I tell you that if two of you on earth agree about anything they ask for, it will be done for them by my Father in heaven." (Matthew 18:19)*

Why do you think Satan has pulled out all stops to keep the church divided and fighting all over the world? He knows that if we can get our act together long enough to put all our petty differences aside and unite in prayer and worship as the one Bride of Christ that we are – then all heaven will break lose on our streets and Satan will lose thousands of prisoners every day!

So, the enemy of God continues to divide and conquer. Until we finally wake up to this and stop playing into Satan's hands, we will not see the Kingdom of God manifest in our city or nation in any significant and tangible way.

CHAPTER FIVE
The Spirit Comes in Power

As we continue this study in the book of Acts, we now come to what is undoubtedly the most read and most quoted section of Luke's account of the birth and growth of the church.

> *"When the day of Pentecost came, they were all together in one place. Suddenly a sound like the blowing of a violent wind came from heaven and filled the whole house where they were sitting.*
>
> *They saw what seemed to be tongues of fire that separated and came to rest on each of them. All of them were filled with the Holy Spirit and began to speak in other tongues as the Spirit enabled them."* (Acts 2:1-4)

Pentecost is translated from the Greek *pentekoste* which means *fiftieth* and it marked the annual Jewish festival scheduled for fifty days after the Passover. It was also called the 'The Feast of Weeks' and the 'The Feast of Harvest' because on that day Jewish people presented the first fruits of their annual harvest.

Was it a coincidence for the Holy Spirit to bring the necessary power for the disciples to be witnesses to Jesus throughout the world precisely on the day of thanksgiving for the harvest? Possibly, but perhaps not. The disciples were about to begin reaping a harvest of souls that has continued now for over 2,000 years. Do you remember what Jesus said about the harvest?

> *"Do you not say, 'Four months more and then the harvest'? I tell you, open your eyes and look at the fields! They are ripe for harvest. Even now the reaper draws his wages, even now he harvests the crop for eternal life, so that the sower and the reaper may be glad together."* (John 4:35-36)

> *"The harvest is plentiful but the workers are few. Ask the Lord of the harvest, therefore, to send out workers into his harvest field."* (Matthew 9:37-38)

What were the disciples praying for with one accord in one place? They were praying for the Holy Spirit to come upon them and impart to them the power to do what Jesus had asked them to do - and that is to bring the gospel of God's grace to people right across the world - across all conceivable barriers. They were praying that the Lord would send them forth as labourers into the harvest field.

Missions expert, Donald McGavran, talked about the need to develop a 'theology of harvest.' He was rather impatient with missionaries or evangelists who seem satisfied to search for the lost with little or no regard to how they are ultimately found. Too many Christian workers have seen so little fruit and in order to justify their existence, they develop a rationale for their ministry which doesn't depend on numbers or converts. Results therefore become irrelevant in evaluating success or failure.

Fortunately for us, those disciples in the upper room were not familiar with such a contrived theology. They were praying for something much more positive. They knew that Jesus came to save the lost and they knew that it was God's intent to empower, strengthen and multiply His churches until all people on earth have had the chance to hear the gospel from their own people, who speak their own language and whose word is unobstructed by cultural barriers. This is 'harvest theology.'

Presumably, all of the 120 believers were together in the same house when the Holy Spirit came. We are not sure whether the house was the upper room or some other house in the temple grounds, because they were spending time daily in each of these places. Because of the large place that would have been needed to accommodate the crowd that would have gathered, it was most likely a structure of some kind connected to the temple.

Now I think it is significant that the phrase back in Acts 1:14 is repeated here, telling us that they were *all together in one accord,* as some translations put it. This reminds us of the important need for agreement in prayer. When the Holy Spirit came, there was no room for doubt that it was a unique occasion.

Nothing like this had ever happened when Jesus was on earth. God showed them clearly what Jesus meant when He said it would be to their advantage to have the Holy Spirit with them instead of the Son. Three tangible signs indicated that the Spirit had come. We see the first sign in verse 2.

> *"Suddenly a sound like the blowing of a violent wind came from heaven and filled the whole house where they were sitting."*
> *(Acts 2:2)*

The sound must have been tremendous. Those of us who live in areas that are largely protected from windstorms, tornadoes and hurricanes will not appreciate what strong winds really are, nor the sound they make.

The sound must have been public and external and not just a phenomenon of group psychologically. It was loud enough, unusual enough and probably terrifying enough, so that the people in the temple area of Jerusalem and other parts of the city were drawn toward this to see what might be happening. In our day it would have made the evening news!

I want to focus for a moment on the word 'suddenly.' The Holy Spirit is free and sovereign and not bound to anyone's timing or technique for how to get His power.

We should be confident of His daily, indwelling presence and grace, walk in the obedience of this faith, and pray always for the outpouring of power from on high. But we cannot make the Spirit come and when He comes, He often comes suddenly. He will never become anyone's servant. He loves and He serves, but He keeps his own hours. He knows what is best for us.

In 1871, two women in Dwight L. Moody's congregation felt an unusual burden to pray for Moody "*that the Lord would give him the baptism of the Holy Ghost and of fire.*" Moody would see them praying in the front row of his church and he was irritated. He eventually gave in and in September began to pray with them every Friday afternoon. He felt like his ministry was becoming a sounding brass with little power.

On November 24, 1871, Moody's church building was destroyed in the great Chicago fire. He went to New York to seek financial help. Day and night he would walk the streets desperate for the touch of God's power in his life.

Then suddenly this happened to Moody, and I quote:

> *"One day, in the city of New York - oh, what a day! - I cannot describe it, I seldom refer to it; it is almost too sacred an experience to name ... I can only say that God revealed himself to me, and I had such an experience of his love that I had to ask him to stay his hand. I went to preaching again. The sermons were not different; I did not present any new truths, and yet hundreds were converted. I would not now be placed back where I was before that blessed experience if you should give me all the world - it would be small dust in the balance."*

He prayed, he obeyed and he waited. But he did not make the Spirit come. He came suddenly and when He came, notice that the effect was Pentecostal - not this time in the experience of tongues, but in the harvest. When the Spirit comes in power, He comes suddenly - on His own terms and in His own time - and He comes for harvesting.

> *"They saw what seemed to be tongues of fire that separated and came to rest on each of them."* (Acts 2:3)

The first tangible sign was audible, the second was visual. At presumably the same time they heard the sound of the wind, the disciples actually saw 120 separate tongues of fire touch each person's head. At that moment, John the Baptist's prophecy about Jesus started to unfold. Do you remember the prophecy from John the Baptist?

> *"John answered them all, "I baptize you with water. But one who is more powerful than I will come, the straps of whose sandals I am not worthy to untie. He will baptize you with the Holy Spirit and fire."* (Luke 3:16)

Moses also experienced God's presence in the burning bush and Isaiah's lips were touched with the burning coal of holiness from the altar. Dr John White was one of the greatest Christian authors of the 20th century and my wife and I were given the incredible privilege of spending a whole week living with and learning from Dr White in a special Pastor's Retreat thirty years ago. Let me share with you something which John wrote about his encounter with the Holy Spirit:

> "On one occasion it was as I prayed with the elders and deacons in my home. I had tried to teach them what worship was ... We then turned to prayer. Perhaps partly to be a model to them I began to express worship, conscious of the poverty of my words. Then suddenly I saw in front of me a column of flame of about two feet in width. It seemed to arise from beneath the floor and to pass through the ceiling of the room. I knew - without being told - knew by some infallible kind of knowing that transcended the use of my intellect, that I was in the presence of the God of holiness. In stunned amazement I watched a rising column of flames in our own living room, while my brothers remained with their heads quietly bowed and their eyes closed...
>
> I felt that I was in the presence of reality and that my brothers were asleep. For years afterward I never spoke of the incident. The others who were present could not have perceived the blend of stark terror and joy that threatened to sweep me away. How could I live and see what I saw? Garbled words of love and of worship tumbled out of my mouth as I struggled to hang on to my self-control. I was no longer trying to worship; worship was undoing me, pulling me apart. And to be pulled apart was both terrifying and full of glory."
> (When the Spirit Comes with Power, p. 87–88)

This is what happened, it seems, to the disciples in Acts 2 when they saw tongues of fire and heard the violent wind. It filled them with an overwhelming sense of the presence of God. Until that moment we can imagine them praying (Acts 1:14) and reciting to each other the 23rd Psalm. Then suddenly something happens that utterly transforms their knowledge of God's presence into an *experience* of God's presence!

They see fire on each other's heads and they hear a loud wind. They are filled not merely with a deductive certainty of God's present reality based on their knowledge of Him, but with an experiential certainty based on the extraordinary outpouring of the Holy Spirit.

The fire begins to burn in their hearts (Luke 24:32) and in their mouths ("tongues of fire"), and the sound of the wind surrounds them and envelops them with the tokens of God's power. They are simply overwhelmed with the greatness of God and it begins to spill out in praise. Like John White, they are almost undone by worship - so much so that some people say they're drunk (v. 13). Perhaps at this point they may have remembered Jesus' promise:

> *"Very truly I tell you, whoever believes in me will do the works I have been doing, and they will do even greater things than these, because I am going to the Father." (John 14:12)*

Some people struggle with the "greater things than these" part of this promise. How could anyone do greater works than Jesus Christ, they ask. The answer lies in the fact that the power by which Jesus ministered is the same power available to all of His disciples, then and now. Jesus was anointed by the same Spirit that you and I and all believers are filled with and empowered by. Once we realise that it's God the Holy Spirit Who performs these mighty feats, we realise that He can minister in this way at any time and through anyone He wishes. That's why Jesus could promise what He did about our greater works.

> *"All of them were filled with the Holy Spirit and began to speak in other tongues as the Spirit enabled them." (Acts 2:4)*

To me it is interesting that the first miracle recorded after Jesus went home to heaven, is a miracle that, as far as we know, the Holy Spirit never did through Jesus. To our knowledge, Jesus never spoke in a language which He did not learn - but the disciples did. In fact, between them, they spoke in at least 15 different languages which they had never learned, and were understood by those who spoke them as their native language!

Luke lists 15 language groups but there is no reason to assume that this is a complete list. It may just be a representative list. Luke may have simply listed these groups as a 'for example' just to explain the magnitude of this miracle. It seems strange, for example, that none are mentioned from Greece or Syria. The Jewish Talmud reported that there were 70 nations in the Jewish dispersion and because Luke said people had come from every nation under heaven, it is probable that many more than fifteen language groups were present.

Although most of them would have been Hellenistic Jews, a number of them were also proselytes, according to verse 10. The Proselytes were Gentiles by birth who have converted to Judaism by going through the required ceremonies including baptism and circumcision for males.

> "Then how is it that each of us hears them in our native language?" (Acts 2:8)

From the time Jesus that was baptised to this point in history, virtually all the evangelism that was recorded in the Bible was mono-cultural, or as I explained in chapter one, E1 evangelism. There were no significant barriers for the gospel to cross.

The Apostles could have preached to the crowd in Aramaic and communicated fairly well. Those among them who knew Greek, could have done the same. But God had other plans to cross what we now see as a formidable cultural barrier. He did something that is certainly not an established missiological pattern - but it is a principle. God took steps to contextualise the gospel. That is, make it relevant to the receiving culture. He showed that He respected the culture and language of each and every one of the people groups who had gathered there.

The method He used was to perform this miracle of languages that allowed the disciples to speak in dialects that they had never learned. The first principle of cross-cultural evangelism is always to present the gospel of Jesus Christ in cultural forms that are appropriate to each people group. God certainly did that here!

For example, if you wanted to get the gospel into an untouched tribe in the heart of Africa, you wouldn't walk into their village with an NIV Bible tucked under your arm and start preaching in English on the nearest street corner! And if you wanted to reach the youth culture right here in our own nation you would not invite them into a grand old cathedral, fire up the pipe organ and sing *Nearer My God to Thee*.

That is why Bible translation work and language studies are seen as more important today than at any other time in the history of global missions. We must get the good news to people in a way they can understand and embrace. That was a very easy sentence to write, but it represents the single greatest challenge facing the church today, if we truly want to fulfill the Great Commission.

If we are really serious about doing what God has called us to do and being who God has called us to be, then each of us needs to be prepared to make a commitment to learning, understanding and growing the mission of Christ and embracing the part He expects us to play in the fulfillment of that mission. What I'm writing now can and will change your life and your whole understanding of the church. But that cannot and will not happen unless you make a choice to be informed and interested and willing to step out in faith and be challenged by God.

I'm reminded of the man who was conducting a survey in his city. He approached one man on the footpath and asked him what he thought were the two greatest problems in the world. The man kept walking and said, *"I don't know and I don't care."* Little did he know, his answer was absolutely spot on. It could be argued that ignorance and apathy are the two greatest problems in the world today. We need to be informed; we desperately need teaching; we need to learn about God; about ourselves; about our reason for being here; about God's intention for us for this world - and we need to really care. We need to be interested and concerned and dare I say it, we also need to be passionate about life and ministry and the purposes of God. None of that will happen without power from on high.

CHAPTER SIX
Inadequacy Meets Sufficiency

None of us like to feel inadequate, but I suggest that a sense of our own inadequacy is actually a gift. To recognise that we have a need may be the first step in seeing that need met. Feeling our own inability or insufficiency may seem like a negative thing, when in fact it may be quite the opposite.

There is a notion in our contemporary culture that recognising our own inability or insufficiency is somehow contrary to the principles of success. Self-confident, high-powered, aggressive personalities seem to be the big winners in the world today. The truth is, most of us simply don't live there. We may well put on a facade in order to appear confident and assertive, but in actual fact, we often feel just the opposite. We are worried about the future; we are worried about the present; trying to balance job and family; trying to be good parents and providers, good role models, good wives and husbands. Sometimes it is really tough and many times, we just feel totally inadequate.

Imagine how the Apostles felt in the days preceding Pentecost. For several years they had really been living an awesome life with Jesus. They were following one of the most exciting figures of all of human history. Every single day they were experiencing the miraculous; they were listening to the most insightful teacher of truth who had ever appeared on our planet. It was indeed a time for high adventure.

Then came His senseless murder. Can you imagine the despair and defeat that must have gripped their hearts? But then He rose from the dead and appeared to them a number of times. What an exhilarating experience that would have been! But now they have lost Jesus again (so they thought) when He ascended to the right hand of the Father. Jesus had challenged them with what we refer to as The Great Commission, but He had told them to go to Jerusalem and wait. I'm sure they didn't quite understand what that meant.

But wait they did and as they waited, a terrible truth would have gripped their hearts. Jesus is gone! This powerful figure around whom their whole lives had been built for so long was now gone and they were alone. Certainly, they had each other, but it wasn't the same without Jesus. Just imagine how they felt.

I'm sure they had lots of questions: *'What would it be like now? Who among them could ever fill His shoes? How could they ever fulfil His Great Commission? Was this all a big dream? Was it now over?'* Questions, many questions, but no answers. Whatever else they thought or felt, I am sure they felt empty. This man Who had filled their lives was gone and they were incredibly empty. This sense of emptiness is shared by many people today. Even many Christians feel empty. There is something missing in their lives; something they can't quite put their finger on. But they recognise a real need. They feel the need for power in their own personal lives. They feel the need for a sense of adequacy.

I'm sure all of the Apostles felt that need, especially one. Peter is a prime example of the spiritual pilgrimage of many Christians. He went through what many of us have gone through or are going through. Perhaps as we focus on what happened to Peter, we will see the principles behind the power which completely changed his life and can impact our lives the same way. Facing our inadequacy doesn't sound like an exciting thing to do, but in many ways it's the first step to a fulfilled life. It was for Peter. He needed it desperately and it can be a first step for us as we face our inadequacy.

Peter was a most appealing character but he was just an ordinary guy. There was nothing extraordinary about his life. He was just a fisherman. He and his father and brothers had built a fishing business. Every day they went to work. Every day they faced the pressures of the marketplace. He wasn't overly educated. He didn't belong to the elite social class. He was just like you and me. When Jesus called him, he responded. He didn't really know what that meant. He wasn't really aware of all the implications of following Jesus, just as we are not aware when we come to Him. But the desire was certainly there.

He wanted to follow the Lord and, in many ways, he felt like he could follow him well. Peter was an impulsive kind of guy. He was fairly confident in his own abilities and many times he bit off more than he could chew. He had many lessons to learn, one of the most important being - Peter could not do it on his own.

Peter had to come face to face with his own inadequacy just as we must. This was going to be essential for his future spiritual growth. We find the account in Mark 14. Jesus has been arrested and Peter follows from a distance. He is interested to see what will happen to Jesus. Peter thinks he is one of the Lord's most faithful followers, and perhaps he is. But he is about to come face to face with his own inadequacy.

> *"While Peter was below in the courtyard, one of the servant girls of the high priest came by. When she saw Peter warming himself, she looked closely at him. "You also were with that Nazarene, Jesus," she said. But he denied it. "I don't know or understand what you're talking about," he said, and went out into the entryway. When the servant girl saw him there, she said again to those standing around, "This fellow is one of them." Again, he denied it.*
>
> *After a little while, those standing near said to Peter, "Surely you are one of them, for you are a Galilean." He began to call down curses, and he swore to them, "I don't know this man you're talking about." Immediately the rooster crowed the second time. Then Peter remembered the word Jesus had spoken to him: "Before the rooster crows twice you will disown me three times." And he broke down and wept."* (Mark 14:66-72)

Peter was headstrong and he thought he would never deny his Lord. Now he had. In fact, he had denied Him three times. He didn't even have the courage to stand up before a servant girl and confess his faith in Christ. He wasn't willing to identify himself with the Saviour. How could he do such a thing? I'm sure he was filled with frustration, shame and a deep sense of failure. Disappointment was too weak a word. Total discouragement is far better, perhaps even utter despair.

I'm sure these are all emotions Peter must have felt. His heart must have ached. The Scripture says that he wept bitterly. Peter had come face to face with the reality of his own inadequacy. The irony was that he truly did not want to deny his Lord. Yet, as Jesus had said only a few short hours before, "*The spirit is willing but the flesh is weak.*" Peter did not want to deny his Lord, yet he had. "*Oh, God, how could I have done such a thing? I said I would never deny you and I have done the very thing I said I would never do! What's the matter with me? Oh, God, I'm a failure.*"

Have you ever felt that way? I'm sure you have. It's common to all of us. In our jobs, or at home, and in ministry, many times we come face to face with our own inadequacy and failure. It's not very encouraging and we all feel a deep sense of frustration at times at our efforts to follow Jesus. Call it the frustration index if you like. The frustration index is the amount of tension we feel as we face the gap between what we know to do and our actual performance.

When the level of our spiritual knowledge is high, but our level of performance low, there is a real tension created, a sense of frustration felt as we recognise that we are not living up to our own understanding of what God expects of us and what we also expect of ourselves. Eventually, we must come face to face with our own inadequacy. Peter did, and so must we. It may be the very thing we need. Facing our own inadequacy is good for us - it prepares us for God's work in our lives.

Someone once said, "*God only fills empty vessels.*" There is a real sense in which that is true. What we may need is to come to a place of emptying in our own lives. We may need to come to a place of brokenness. That may be the very thing we need, to give us the right perspective for our lives - the perspective we need in order for God to begin His best work in us, like He did for Peter.

That may be the preparation for our personal Pentecost. It was for the apostles and for Peter. It can be for us. Let's have another look at the opening verses of Acts chapter 2.

"When the day of Pentecost came, they were all together in one place. Suddenly a sound like the blowing of a violent wind came from heaven and filled the whole house where they were sitting. They saw what seemed to be tongues of fire that separated and came to rest on each of them. All of them were filled with the Holy Spirit and began to speak in other tongues as the Spirit enabled them." (Acts 2:1-4)

Only by facing our inadequacy will we truly encounter His sufficiency. That is what Pentecost was. It was an encounter with God. This is its real significance. Be careful not to miss that in the details and drama of this story. The real significance of Pentecost is not the rushing, mighty wind or the visible tongues of fire, or even the fact that they spoke in many other languages. The real significance of Pentecost is that broken, inadequate human beings had an encounter with God.

God showed up and by His Spirit, God took over! They were filled with God's Spirit and clothed with power from on high, just as Jesus had promised. Pentecost means that God is in charge.

What happened at Pentecost was a transforming event. Like the caterpillar which spins its cocoon and waits there while an inner work of transformation takes place, so the disciples were waiting as God did His unseen work in their hearts to prepare them for that day. Then as the caterpillar emerges, something wonderful has happened. He is no longer a caterpillar, but a beautiful new creation. His life has been changed. He has been completely transformed.

On the day of Pentecost, God came in power and changed the lives of a multitude. Like the caterpillar, they would never be the same again. They certainly didn't act the same. Accused of being intoxicated, they were doing strange things. They weren't acting like normal people. They were not drunk with wine; they were drunk with the Spirit of God. They were overwhelmed by the presence and power of God Himself. That's precisely what we need today. That is what the church needs today.

As we embrace our insufficiency and own it, we will encounter His sufficiency and understand the dynamic of how we should live. Pentecost was an encounter with the sufficiency of God. They had been emptied only to be filled. It finally had clicked; it all made sense now. They understood how to live above the level of their own inadequacy. They must learn to depend upon His sufficiency. They must learn to live in His power.

That is certainly what we need today. We need our own personal Pentecost because, as we encounter God, we will find the power to live our lives as God intended. Facing our inadequacy not only brings us to a place of encountering His sufficiency, but both taken together, it produces a supernatural ability to live the dynamic life Jesus died to give us. That happened to Peter.

> *"Then Peter stood up with the Eleven, raised his voice and addressed the crowd: "Fellow Jews and all of you who live in Jerusalem, let me explain this to you; listen carefully to what I say." (Acts 2:14)*

Something has changed! This is a very different Peter. A few days prior to this, he could not even admit before a servant girl around a campfire that he even knew Jesus. He had acted like a coward. And now, with multiplied thousands gathered together, he dares to stand up and command the attention of the entire crowd. Something has happened. This is not the Peter we knew! What has happened to this man? Pentecost happened.

Encountering God's enabling power is what happened. Being filled with the Spirit is what happened. A total transformation is what happened. Peter appears different because he *is* different. Indeed, something incredible has happened to this man. He is now operating, not in his own ability, but in God's sufficiency. He is moving by the power of God. God is in charge now. The Holy Spirit is in control, and this is precisely what will produce dynamic, authentic Christian living. It is living in the power, the *dúnamis* of God. That is what Jesus expects of us all. Peter's cowardice had been turned into confidence and his confidence now was in Christ, not himself.

Peter began to understand what Paul would write later, *"I can do all things through Christ who strengthens me."* This was the result of encountering the very presence of Christ. In Acts 4, we find Peter and John before the religious leaders and it is said of them:

> *"When they saw the courage of Peter and John and realised that they were unschooled, ordinary men, they were astonished and they took note that these men had been with Jesus."* (Acts 4:13)

Encountering the presence of Jesus Christ is what will give us confidence. It is the confidence of knowing that He indwells us by His Spirit, that He empowers us by His Spirit, that He lives in us and through us by His Spirit. Indeed, it was a life-changing experience for all.

At Pentecost, 3,000 people came to know Christ, and the church was born in Jerusalem. It was a dynamic church, filled with dynamic people who were living out their Christianity in the midst of a secular society.

This is the picture of a living, dynamic fellowship of believers who are empowered by the Holy Spirit of God. These are people who have seen their own inadequacy. They have encountered the sufficiency of God and because they have been filled with His Spirit, they are now empowered to live dynamically changed lives in the midst of a society which runs counter to the principles of God's Word. It is a church made up of ordinary people, living extraordinary lives by the power of the Spirit of God.

Have you come face to face with your inadequacy? Perhaps you have. Maybe you even feel it keenly today. Don't despair - there is hope. It may be just the place God has brought you to. He may be bringing you to the point where you can be filled with His grace and love and power. God loves to fill empty vessels!

If you sense your inadequacy today, come to Him and allow Him to fill you with Himself. As you encounter His sufficiency, you will be empowered to live dynamically. You will experience the power of God just like those early disciples did.

Imagine having your heart filled with God's love, your mind full of His truth, your soul full of faith and His goodness, and having courage and boldness without fear. Imagine sensing His real presence, knowing He is in the room with you, and your heart sensing His tender promptings and knowing what to say or do in your own life and in the ministry of serving others.

That's what the presence of the Spirit provides for us: the privilege to be filled with God's love and to be empowered by Him as we are given supernatural ability. The greatest need of every Christian and every church fellowship today is a sustained consciousness of the personal presence and power of the Living God.

Like the power of a volcano pouring forth fiery lava, the power of God poured forth on the followers of Jesus gathered in Jerusalem on the day of Pentecost around 33 A.D. Born that day was a radically new creation on earth that never existed before - the church - born not by natural power but by supernatural power. And the power behind its existence is the Holy Spirit Who is a radical blessing to every believer and to the world - having a profound and far-reaching effect.

We can look at Peter's seemingly ordinary life and see that it was very valuable to God. His value certainly did not come from being super-educated, wealthy, handsome, or a star athlete in the ancient world.

Peter was just an ordinary man who knew his weaknesses but yielded to the Spirit's transforming power to do whatever Jesus wanted him to do. He knew that he was dearly loved by His Saviour.

God made Peter to be loyal, open-hearted, and verbally gifted. He used those very traits to further His gospel message. God transformed Peter's impulsiveness, fearfulness, and tendency to be weak-willed into a man who carefully sought guidance from the Lord, trusted the Lord, and was bold in doing what Christ called him to do. The Lord can do exactly the same for you.

When Jesus commissioned His followers to go into the world and make disciples (Matthew 28:19), that declaration was given to ordinary, everyday women and men like you and me. None of them were ordained preachers, hired church staff, or leaders of missionary organizations. Some did extraordinary things and are written about in the book of Acts. Many others were simply proclaiming the good news wherever they went. These were unnamed, ordinary people, sharing Jesus with family, friends, and neighbours in the context of their ordinary, everyday lives. They allowed the Holy Spirit to transform them into Christ's followers who resembled Christ more than their old selves. They dared to be different from their world - and God blessed that.

It's okay to be ordinary. It's okay to admit your inadequacy. God is actually attracted to weakness. He just cannot resist those who humbly and honestly admit how desperately they need Him. It is our weakness, our inadequacy, our emptiness which makes room for His strength and sufficiency.

Our willingness to let the Spirit of God control and transform us requires us to recognize that we are too weak to do anything of spiritual significance on our own. Then, He takes over and uses all the gifts He has given us for God's glory. The God of the unexpected takes every day, ordinary kinds of people like you and me and He works through our weakness, leads us to trust Him more, and surprises us with gifts from unexpected sources. Our God uses the ordinary and unexpected to accomplish His purposes. What a joy it is to serve Him!

CHAPTER SEVEN
The Church's First Sermon

Apparently, one of the greatest fears people have is the fear of speaking in public. It even ranks ahead of the fear of death! Can you imagine that fear increasing if you knew that you would be speaking to a hostile audience? Add to that the fact that the audience is not just a small group, but at least five thousand hostile people, and you must address them without a modern sound system. This is the stuff of nightmares!

To make matters worse, you have made a fool of yourself only weeks before in such a way that many people in your audience would have heard about it. You would also have no time to prepare your message. The opportunity presents itself and you're on – without any warning, without any notes!

Such was the situation facing the Apostle Peter on the Day of Pentecost. The sound of the rushing wind from heaven had drawn a large crowd, which then heard all the believers speaking of the great deeds of God in the many different native languages of the crowd. This perplexed them and some were very curious, while others were mocking:

> *"Amazed and perplexed, they asked one another, "What does this mean?" Some, however, made fun of them and said, "They have had too much wine." (Acts 2:12-13)*

It was to this Jewish crowd in the city of Jerusalem, where Jesus had been killed just only weeks before, that Peter delivered the sermon which launched the church as we know it. In terms of a response - about 3,000 came to Christ just that day! Clearly, an effective sermon!

Luke only gives us some of that great sermon (see 2:40). But even so, there is far more here than I can deal with adequately in one chapter, but I will give it a shot and hope that you might do some personal study later.

I want to walk you through this sermon, explaining the flow of thought so that you grasp Peter's method and argument. Even though you may never be called upon to preach to a crowd, you will have opportunities to bear witness for Christ. Studying Peter's sermon may help you to be ready.

> "Then Peter stood up with the Eleven, raised his voice and addressed the crowd: "Fellow Jews and all of you who live in Jerusalem, let me explain this to you; listen carefully to what I say. These people are not drunk, as you suppose. It's only nine in the morning! No, this is what was spoken by the prophet Joel:
>
> "'In the last days, God says, I will pour out my Spirit on all people. Your sons and daughters will prophesy, your young men will see visions, your old men will dream dreams. Even on my servants, both men and women, I will pour out my Spirit in those days, and they will prophesy.
>
> I will show wonders in the heavens above and signs on the earth below, blood and fire and billows of smoke. The sun will be turned to darkness and the moon to blood before the coming of the great and glorious day of the Lord. And everyone who calls on the name of the Lord will be saved." (Acts 2:14-21)

Peter begins with the questions that the crowd was asking about the phenomena of Pentecost, linking what they saw and heard to the prophecy of Joel 2:28-32. He then changes focus abruptly:

> "Fellow Israelites, listen to this: Jesus of Nazareth was a man accredited by God to you by miracles, wonders and signs, which God did among you through him, as you yourselves know. This man was handed over to you by God's deliberate plan and foreknowledge; and you, with the help of wicked men, put him to death by nailing him to the cross. But God raised him from the dead, freeing him from the agony of death, because it was impossible for death to keep its hold on him.
>
> David said about him: "'I saw the Lord always before me. Because he is at my right hand, I will not be shaken.

Therefore, my heart is glad and my tongue rejoices; my body also will rest in hope, because you will not abandon me to the realm of the dead, you will not let your holy one see decay. You have made known to me the paths of life; you will fill me with joy in your presence.'

"Fellow Israelites, I can tell you confidently that the patriarch David died and was buried, and his tomb is here to this day. But he was a prophet and knew that God had promised him on oath that he would place one of his descendants on his throne.

Seeing what was to come, he spoke of the resurrection of the Messiah, that he was not abandoned to the realm of the dead, nor did his body see decay. God has raised this Jesus to life, and we are all witnesses of it. Exalted to the right hand of God, he has received from the Father the promised Holy Spirit and has poured out what you now see and hear. For David did not ascend to heaven, and yet he said,

"The Lord said to my Lord: 'Sit at my right hand until I make your enemies a footstool for your feet.' Therefore, let all Israel be assured of this: God has made this Jesus, whom you crucified, both Lord and Messiah." (Acts 2:22-36)

Peter makes it very clear that God authenticated Jesus as Lord and Christ (2:36). But he builds his argument inductively (a good method with hostile audiences), building his case point by point, but not giving the main point until last.

When his audience responds with conviction of sin, asking, *"What shall we do?"* Peter tells them to repent and be baptized, and 3,000 did so. Let's work through his sermon in more detail:

1. *Joel prophesied about the outpouring of the Holy Spirit that you have just witnessed (2:14-21)*

Notice that Peter appeals twice to his audience to listen carefully to his words (2:14,22). No matter how dynamic the speaker may be, the audience has a responsibility to listen carefully. Even the Lord Jesus, the most gifted speaker in history, exhorted His audiences to take care how they listened (Luke 8:18).

In other words, the responsibility for a good sermon lies not only with the preacher, but also with the hearers. We should always ask God to give us ears to hear what He wants to say to us at that point through His Word.

Peter begins with a touch of humour. Some mockers were accusing the believers who spoke in tongues of being drunk with wine. Peter could have ignored them or responded defensively, but instead he says, in effect, *"It's too early for us to be drunk!"* The Jews would not normally have eaten or drunk at this hour during the Feast of Pentecost.

Then Peter explains that the phenomena they had seen and heard is, *"what was spoken of through the prophet Joel"* (2:16). He proceeds to quote, with a few minor variations, Joel 2:28-32. Later Peter will cite Psalm 16:8-11 and Psalm 110:1. He did not have a Bible in book form, since books as we know them were not even invented. And he did not unroll several scrolls to the right text so that he could read these verses. Rather, he recited them from memory! Peter's citation of Joel makes three points:

a. *In the last days, God will pour out His Spirit on all people. (2:17-18)*

Joel's prophecy actually says, "after this," but Peter changes it to "the last days." The time from Jesus' first coming until His second coming can all be referred to as the last days.

The Apostles did not know that it would stretch out over 2,000 years. But as Paul put it, we are the ones *"upon whom the ends of the ages have come"* (1 Corinthians 10:11). Peter warned,

> *"… in the last days mockers will come with their mocking, following after their own lusts, and saying, 'Where is the promise of His coming?'"* (2 Peter 3:3-4)

He goes on to say that with the Lord, one day is like a thousand years, and a thousand years like one day. But Peter's citation of Joel is simply making the point, we are now in the end times when this prophecy will be fulfilled.

Peter's use of Joel is consistent with what biblical scholars have identified from the Dead Sea Scrolls as a typical form of Hebrew teaching, called a 'pesher' (taken from the Hebrew word for 'interpretation'). Peter never specifically shows how prophecy, visions, and dreams are identified with the phenomenon of speaking in tongues that everyone had heard. But he seems to use this passage since it is the nearest equivalent to tongues in Old Testament phraseology.

Peter's main point is not the particular form that the outpouring of the Spirit took, but rather that the Spirit was poured out *"on all flesh,"* not just the prophets or rabbis, but even the sons and daughters would experience this outpouring of the Spirit (2:17). Not just the older men, but also younger men would know the Lord and His will ('visions'). Not just the wealthy, but even bondslaves would know the fulness of the Spirit. Not just men, but also women would have the Spirit. As the apostle Paul later wrote to the believers in Corinth:

> *"… by one Spirit we were all baptized into one body, whether Jews or Greeks, whether slaves or free, and we were all made to drink of one Spirit" (1 Corinthians 12:13).*

Therefore, no believer today lacks the presence of the indwelling Holy Spirit. Everyone can experience the same phenomenon.

    b)   *This outpouring of the Spirit will be followed by a time of judgement. (2:19-20)*

Peter did not know how soon these judgments would take place (since Joel does not indicate such). He was not claiming that they had been fulfilled on the Day of Pentecost; rather, he is saying that these things would precede *"the great and glorious day of the Lord."* Since the prophecy had begun to be fulfilled, as evidenced by the outpouring of the Holy Spirit, it is reasonable to assume that the rest will come to pass in due time.

Some relate these signs in the heavens back to the darkening of the sky on the day of Jesus' crucifixion, understanding them as tokens of the advent of the day of the Lord.

Others have interpreted the signs as symbols for any cataclysmic judgments, whether volcanoes, earthquakes, fires, or whatever. But Revelation 6:12 predicts these same signs when the Lamb breaks the sixth seal during the Great Tribulation. Thus, the literal fulfillment still awaits that time just prior to the return of Christ. Peter's point is that the outpouring of the Spirit predicted by Joel has happened. The Messianic age has begun. Then Joel offers good news:

c)   *Everyone who calls on the name of the Lord will be saved. (2:21)*

Here is the great mercy of our God! He offers to those who deserve His judgment a means of escape. Whoever will call on the name of the Lord will be saved.

Up to this point, Peter has been rather generic. He has linked the phenomena of Pentecost to Joel's prophecy about the outpouring of God's Spirit in the last days. This hints that the day of the Messiah has now dawned, inaugurating the last days, but he hasn't yet said that clearly.

He has also brought up the subject of God's judgment at the final Day of the Lord, but he hasn't stated yet that his audience (good religious Jews) need to fear that judgment. And he has set forth the offer of God's mercy for anyone who will take it.

But now he shifts from preaching to meddling! He gets specific about just who this Lord is, upon Whom a person must call to be saved. He shows them that they had crucified their Messiah!

2. *God authenticated Jesus as both Lord and Christ (2:22-36)*

Although he doesn't drop the punch line until verse 36, Peter shows four ways that God authenticated Jesus as Lord and the Christ (Messiah):

a.   *God authenticated Jesus as Lord and Christ through His miracles. (2:22)*

Even the enemies of Jesus had to accept the stark reality of His miracles (although some attributed them to Satan's power - Luke 11:15). Most people acknowledged, as Nicodemus did, that *"no one can do these signs that You do unless God is with him"* (John 3:2). Peter reminds his audience that Jesus had done many such miracles in their midst, and they knew it.

While many in our day deny that miracles can occur, they are basing their denials on the assumption that God does not exist, contrary to much evidence in creation. The miracles that Jesus performed, attested and affirmed by eyewitnesses, including His enemies (John 11:47), authenticate Him as Lord and Christ.

   b. *God authenticated Jesus as Lord and Christ through His death. (2:23)*

Here Peter treads on a number of toes: *"This man, delivered over by the predetermined plan and foreknowledge of God, you nailed to a cross by the hands of godless men and put Him to death."* Jesus' death at first glance may have seemed like something that invalidated His messianic claims. But Peter shows that Jesus was not killed because He was a victim of His enemies. He was killed because God predetermined before the world began that Jesus would die as the Saviour of His people.

Isaiah 53:10 prophesied, *"But the Lord was pleased to crush Him, putting Him to grief."* And so rather than invalidating Jesus as Lord and Messiah, His death actually validated Him since it was a fulfillment of God's eternal decree.

Does this mean that since God determined it, men are not held responsible? No, Peter says, *"you nailed [Him] to a cross by the hands of lawless men [the Romans] and put Him to death."* Without violating their will, God used evil men to accomplish His eternal purpose, but those evil men were responsible for their crime. No one can blame God for their own sin.

   c. *God authenticated Jesus as Lord and Christ through His resurrection. (2:24-32)*

After spending just one verse each on Jesus' life and death, Peter spends nine verses on His resurrection, which is the main theme of all the apostolic preaching in Acts. Note (2:23-24) the implicit contrast between *"you put Him to death. But God raised Him up again."* In other words, they were guilty of opposing God!

Peter cites Psalm 16:8-11 to show an Old Testament prediction of the resurrection. In that psalm, David declares that God will not abandon His soul to Hades nor allow His holy one to undergo decay. But, Peter argues, David both died and was buried, and his tomb was right there in Jerusalem. In other words, David's body did actually undergo decay.

Therefore, David as a prophet knew that God had promised to seat one of his descendants on his throne, and so he looked ahead and spoke of the resurrection of Christ. Peter identifies Jesus as the Messiah when he confidently states, *"This Jesus, God raised up again, to which we are all witnesses."* (2:32). Perhaps the other eleven standing with Peter nodded in affirmation.

Thus, Jesus' miracles, death and resurrection all authenticate Him as both Lord and Christ. But there is a final piece of evidence:

> d. *God authenticated Jesus as Lord and Christ through His exaltation and the outpouring of the Holy Spirit. (2:33-36)*

Peter states that the ascended, exalted Jesus was the One Who had sent the Holy Spirit as evidenced by the miracle of everyone speaking in foreign languages. Again, he cites David in Psalm 110:1, "The Lord said to my Lord, 'Sit at My right hand until I make your enemies a footstool for your feet.'" Since David is not seated at God's right hand, this must refer to the Messiah. A not-so-subtle implication is that the enemies of the Messiah are those who crucified Him!

Then Peter comes to his punch line in verse 36: "Therefore let all the house of Israel know for certain that God has made Him both Lord and Christ - this Jesus whom you crucified." You can't get much clearer than that!

3. The crowd's response and Peter's application. (2:37-41)

a. The crowd responds with conviction. (2:37)

To be "pierced to the heart" shows their feelings of deep anguish as they realized that they were actually guilty of killing their own Messiah. The Holy Spirit stabbed them with conviction of their terrible sin. Charles Spurgeon once said,

> *"It is idle to attempt to heal those who are not wounded, to attempt to clothe those who have never been stripped, and to make those rich who have never realized their poverty."*

The conviction of sin is often the missing note in our evangelistic efforts. We are too quick in trying to heal people who do not realize how mortally ill they really are. Only after the Spirit of God brings a deep revelation of the reality of their sinful condition, can the gospel of God's amazing grace truly impact them and transform them.

b. Peter applies the message: Repentance, baptism and promise. (2:38-40)

First Peter calls upon them to repent. There are many in our day who argue that repentance has no place in salvation; rather, all a person must do is believe in Christ. Repentance, they say, comes later. If so, Peter botched the gospel! The fact is repentance and faith are flip sides of the same coin. You cannot have true saving faith without repentance.

Others minimize the definition of repentance, saying that it just means to change your mind about who Jesus is. Certainly, it includes that, but it is more than that. Howard Marshall writes, *"The word indicates a change of direction in a person's life rather than simply a mental change of attitude or a feeling of remorse; it signifies a turning away from a sinful and godless way of life."*

Faith in Jesus Christ is implicit in repentance, as it also is in Peter's next word. *"Each of you be baptized in the name of Jesus Christ."* Peter is calling them to an individual response.

Salvation is always a personal transaction, not a group plan. As with John the Baptist's ministry, he links repentance, baptism, and forgiveness of sins (Mark 1:4). Baptism is never just an outward ritual, but rather it's a public confession of one's private faith in and commitment to Jesus Christ.

Those who argue that you must be baptized to be saved use this verse as their proof text. But they ignore both the context of this verse and the overwhelming testimony of Scripture, that salvation is by grace through faith, and that good works (including baptism) are the *result* of salvation (Ephesians 2:8-10).

Granted, the notion of an unbaptized believer was foreign to the Apostles, as it was assumed that saving faith would result in prompt obedience to Jesus Christ. But, in the next chapter (3:19), Peter calls his audience to repent *"so that your sins may be wiped away,"* and never mentions baptism.

When Peter called on them to be baptized, he was asking them to make a radical break with their culture and the religion that had crucified the Messiah, and to be publicly identified with Jesus Christ. This outward symbol would prove the reality of their inward repentance and faith, and the fact that God had forgiven their sins.

Then, Peter proclaims God's promise, that they will receive the gift of the Holy Spirit. When they repented and trusted in Christ, the Holy Spirit was a part of God's gift of salvation. Peter extends the promise beyond them to their children and beyond them to those who are far off, *"as many as the Lord our God will call to Himself."*

While salvation, on the one hand, requires that a person call on the name of the Lord (2:21), on the other hand no one calls on the Lord unless the Lord first calls him/her to Himself (2:39).

Although Peter may not have understood that yet, those who are far off obviously referred to the Gentiles. Luke summarizes Peter's further exhortations with, *"Be saved from this perverse generation"* (2:40). Salvation always demands a radical break from our wicked culture.

c. The result: 3,000 souls brought to Jesus. (2:41)

Much modern evangelism tries to make becoming a Christian as easy as possible. We dodge the issue of sin. We don't talk about the cost of discipleship. We wouldn't dare call on people to make a radical break with their culture. But Peter called these people to repentance and baptism. For a Jew to be baptized was a very traumatic thing. They generally looked on baptism as a rite for Gentile converts or for notorious sinners, not for "good" Jews. But Peter preached it boldly, God worked inwardly, and the church was birthed - 3,000 strong! Peter's sermon in a nutshell was: *Since God has made Jesus both Lord and Christ Who will judge the world, sinners must repent.*

The point of biblical evangelism is not to make people feel good about who they are or to feel that God loves them just as they are (even though that is true). Rather, it is to show them who Jesus Christ truly is, the Lord of the universe, the Christ of God who offered Himself for our sins and who was raised from the dead.

It should show them who they are, sinners who crucified the Son of God, who deserve God's judgment. It should then show them God's great mercy and love, in securing their forgiveness and reconciliation through the life, death and resurrection of Jesus Christ! It should also show them the need to follow Christ and embrace His mission all the days of their life.

CHAPTER EIGHT
Not a Fairy Tale!

"When the people heard this, they were cut to the heart and said to Peter and the other apostles, "Brothers, what shall we do?" Peter replied, "Repent and be baptized, every one of you, in the name of Jesus Christ for the forgiveness of your sins. And you will receive the gift of the Holy Spirit.

The promise is for you and your children and for all who are far off - for all whom the Lord our God will call." With many other words he warned them; and he pleaded with them, "Save yourselves from this corrupt generation." Those who accepted his message were baptized, and about three thousand were added to their number that day." (Acts 2:37-41)

We had a brief look at this passage in the previous chapter, but I want to drill down now and extract some more insights from these verses. Nothing can be as dead, dry, futile and frustrating as church work without the power of the Holy Spirit. On the other hand, nothing is quite as exciting and exhilarating, alive and powerful as a church filled with the Spirit.

The church which was born in the midst of Jerusalem in Acts chapter 2 was certainly such a church. This is not a fairy tale – the church of Jesus Christ was born that day and it was a living, dynamic expression of the power of God to change lives.

We see God at work as the Holy Spirit descends on the day of Pentecost. We see God at work when Peter, a fisher of fish, too cowardly to confess Christ to a servant girl a few days earlier, receives the boldness to become a fisher of men and women. We see God at work, as thousands of people are added to the church from one sermon. We see God changing lives and performing miracles of forgiveness and deliverance in the hearts of His lost children. The church was born that day in Jerusalem, and what a church it was! Through its powerful ministry, the entire world would be changed. It truly was a great and dynamic church.

We want to be part of a church like that, don't we? We want to experience the power and the presence of the Holy Spirit of God. We want to experience the life which comes from a mighty move of the Spirit in our midst.

But we have to ask ourselves what made this first church so powerful? What made it the kind of church God could use? What were the marks of its greatness? What was the character of its people? How is it different from what we see today and what can we do to reconnect with our dynamic roots as the church?

The events leading up to the Day of Pentecost were unique for this small band of disciples of Jesus. They had endured one of the most traumatic and bewildering times of their lives. Jesus had been executed on the cross. The One they believed to be the Messiah had been killed, an innocent man was murdered! They thought it was all over. They didn't know what to do. Then they heard the great news - Jesus was alive! He had risen from the dead. He then appeared to them to confirm this fact.

Even doubting Thomas became a believer. Jesus then told them to wait in Jerusalem for the power of God to come upon them and after that, they would bear witness to Him all over the world. After He said this, Jesus ascended into the clouds right before their very eyes. Wow! What a wild ride that all must have been. I am sure they would have felt every emotion that a person can possibly have.

So, as instructed by Jesus, they went to Jerusalem to wait. They waited and prayed for ten days until the Day of Pentecost, a Jewish feast day, arrived, and God showed up that day. By His Spirit, God poured forth His power on the one hundred and twenty disciples who were waiting as Jesus asked them to.

It was a powerful demonstration of God's presence with tongues of fire hovering above everyone and with everyone speaking in other tongues and the crowd understanding them in a multitude of languages. Something very strange was happening. God had showed up and things were about to change, big time!

One thing that changed was that timid men became bold, one in particular. Peter, a few days before, not able to confess Christ to a servant girl, now stood up before thousands of people and preached a sermon. He was now as bold as a lion and unafraid. He had the power that Jesus had promised. At the conclusion of the sermon, he told them just who Christ really was.

The first mark of a great church is really foundational to all the others. They were a *regenerate* church. In other words, the people in this church had been born again by the Spirit of God. Do you remember this is what Jesus told Nicodemus that every person needed?

> *"I tell you the truth, no one can see the kingdom of God unless he is born again ... You should not be surprised at my saying; you must be born again." (John 3:3,7)*

Jesus came to bring this new birth to people. He came to give us new life by the Holy Spirit. This is what makes all the difference. This is what makes us Christians. We are Christians because we have received this new life. We are made part of the church because we are born from above.

Now that may seem basic, but it is important that we understand this clearly. Far too many people's names have been added to church rolls without ever adding the people to the church. To be in the church of Jesus Christ is no mere formality of adding your name to a roll. To be in His church, you must first be born again. Your spirit must be regenerated by the Spirit of God.

This has not been the practice of every church through history. Some churches have and do admit people to their membership before they make a personal, credible confession of their faith in Jesus Christ. Many are baptised into the local church as babies and grow up thinking that they are Christians because of that ritual which they played no part in whatsoever. But the Scripture nowhere teaches that the application of water on the head of an infant regenerates that child's spirit. The Bible clearly teaches that salvation is by faith. In other words, there must be faith in the heart of the person trusting in Christ.

No one can believe for another person. Each person must come to Christ individually and to lead people to believe that they are okay when they are not, is deception.

Peter has just given a sermon to the Jewish pilgrims in Jerusalem explaining many things to them. First, that the disciples were empowered to speak in various languages to these men from all nations due to the power of the Holy Spirit from God. Second, that Jesus the Nazarene was the Christ sent by God, whom the Jewish people crucified. But His death was planned by God, and now Jesus was resurrected back to life and exalted by God to sit at His right hand.

Furthermore, Jesus had sent the Spirit to empower His followers to live as God intended. These things were prophesied by the prophet Joel and King David, that God's Spirit would work wonders through people, and that God's sent one (the Messiah) would not stay dead but rise to life. Peter then ends his sermon by reminding the Jewish crowd that they are the ones who had called for Jesus' death. They had effectively nailed the Lord and Messiah sent by God to a cross and crucified Him (Acts 2:23,36).

The crowd's response is one of conviction. They did not argue with Peter, or defend themselves, or deny that they had played a role in the death of Jesus the Messiah. They were pierced to the heart; they felt the pain of guilt because what Peter accused them of was true. They put Jesus to death. And this Jesus had really been sent by God after all, and now His power and message was continuing on through the disciples and the Holy Spirit. So, they ask Peter and the rest of the apostles the best question one can ask when convicted of sin, *what shall we do?*

They wanted to know how to make it right. Earlier in Acts 2:5, it is noted that this crowd contained some "reverent" men, despite the fact that they had crucified Jesus. They had been deceived, mistaken, blinded by mob mentality and anger, when they called for the death of the Messiah (Matt. 27:22-26). But they had sinned nonetheless and wanted to make it right. They did not want to linger in their grievous wrongdoing. They are asking Peter how they can fix this.

Peter then shares the good news of Jesus with them - the whole reason that Jesus had willingly and knowingly come to earth to die. The way to fix this was to fix their entire life, from the inside, only by trusting what God could do for them. Peter calls the crowd to repent, which means to confess that they are not right with God and to turn away from their former way of living and turn back to God.

Peter goes on to say that each of them should be baptized in the name of Jesus Christ for the forgiveness of their sins; and they will receive the gift of the Holy Spirit. To be baptized in the name of Jesus Christ means to immerse oneself into water as a symbol of immersing ourselves in Christ. It was a way to show the world that the person who is being baptized is a true follower of Jesus Christ. Their whole life has been transformed by Jesus. Peter says that those who repent and are baptized will receive the gift of the Holy Spirit.

The Spirit created this circumstance to begin with, attracting the crowd of Jewish pilgrims by speaking in their own languages through the remaining followers of Jesus. Now Peter, who has explained that the Spirit is responsible for the miracle that the crowd has witnessed, is telling the crowd that they too will receive this same Spirit. This is because the promise of the Spirit is for you (the crowd) and your children and for all who are far off, as many as the Lord our God will call to Himself.

As we see the spread of the gospel throughout the book of Acts, there are two distinct ways in which the Apostles preach. For the Gentiles, the Apostles call for their listeners to have faith in Jesus to receive the Spirit. And throughout Acts, Gentiles receive the Holy Spirit immediately upon belief. But in these early chapters, the Apostles first call for their Jewish brothers and sisters to repent and to receive the Spirit.

This might be because the Jews are the chosen people. They're already elect, they already believe. But they rejected the Son of God when He came. Now they're called to repent and turn back to God and accept His son, our Saviour.

Throughout the book of Acts, we see Jews receiving the Spirit through repentance and the baptism in keeping with repentance, while Gentiles receive the Holy Spirit immediately upon belief. In the next chapter, Peter will preach again, calling the nation of Israel to repentance, in the hopes that it may bring the Kingdom of Heaven to earth:

> *"Therefore repent and return, so that your sins may be wiped away, in order that times of refreshing may come from the presence of the Lord; and that He may send Jesus, the Christ appointed for you, whom heaven must receive until the period of restoration of all things about which God spoke by the mouth of His holy prophets from ancient time." (Acts 3:19-21)*

Peter is effectively saying, *"If you will repent and if Israel repents, Jesus will return to earth and take the throne of Israel. He's just waiting for you to receive Him."*

This makes clear that if the nation had repented of their rejection of Christ and returned to following God, *"times of refreshing"* would have come by *"the presence of the Lord,"* that God *"may send Jesus,"* meaning Jesus would return and be present among them, for He was *"the Christ appointed"* for Israel, waiting in heaven *"until the period of restoration of all things."*

Here at Pentecost, Peter is calling for this repentance. Ultimately only some Jews repent and follow Jesus (3,000 in this chapter, 5,000 in the next), but not the entire nation, and not its leaders. The time of refreshing and the presence of the Lord was not received. It seems likely that the devastating destruction of the temple in 70 AD was a definitive closing of that window of time when repentance was offered. Jesus returning to earth has not yet happened.

However, the lack of repentance from the Jews provided an immense opportunity for the Gentiles. We are currently in what the Bible refers to as *the time of the Gentiles*, where we are grafted onto the tree of God's chosen people, Israel, through faith in Jesus the Messiah.

God's grace for Israel has extended to the entire world, for those who believe. Non-Jews get to share in Israel's relationship with God, even if the nation itself has rejected Christ. The Apostle Paul addresses this in his letter to the believers in Rome.

> *"... a partial hardening has happened to Israel until the fullness of the Gentiles has come in; and so, all Israel will be saved ..."* (Romans 11:25-26)

Israel has experienced this partial hardening, this stubbornness that keeps them from repentance, but ultimately it is God's will that they shall be saved, for they are His people and His promises are irrevocable.

Peter echoes Jesus' last command to the disciples. Jesus told them to *"be [His] witnesses both in Jerusalem and in all Judea, and Samaria, and as far as the remotest part of the earth"* (Acts 1:8). Now Peter is declaring to the crowd that the Spirit is for the Jews present and far off, for the entirety of the Jewish people spread across the world. The Spirit will come to as many people as the Lord our God will call to Himself; in saying this, Peter acknowledges that it is God who is calling people to Himself, God is pursuing those who are not in a right relationship with Him.

Peter continues to preach this message of repentance. He speaks earnestly and seriously about having seen Jesus rise from the grave, and with many other words he solemnly testified. He then continued to encourage the crowds to change the way they were living and accept God's gift of salvation in Christ. He exhorted them, saying, *"Be saved from this perverse generation!"* This was a warning, for if there is a need to be saved, it is to be saved from something. Peter was calling them to be saved from this perverse generation.

More specifically, the perverse generation of Jewish leaders who led the people of Israel against the Son of God, rather than embrace Him as God's Messiah. They are perverse in the sense that they are incorrect, crooked and corrupt. They are not in submission to God; they do not see clearly; they did not even recognize His Son when He was walking among them speaking the Word of God to them.

Under their leadership, this entire generation of Jews have now become perverse - misled and astray. Peter is calling his audience to repent, to reject the way their current generation is going, and to be saved from the negative consequences that will result from their lack of repentance. Doing so would bring the *"time of refreshing"* when Jesus returns to earth (Acts 3:19-21).

As I have said already, so much present-day evangelism seeks to make coming to Christ easy. Many today would be appalled that Peter made the cost of coming to Christ so high. How could he expect them to turn their backs publicly on their own culture? How could he ask them to risk becoming outcasts among their families and society? How could he demand that they accept as Messiah the very One their leaders had rejected and executed? They would no doubt predict that the results of Peter's sermon would be minimal. That's what we would expect today.

Such was not the case here. The crowd responds powerfully and those who had received his word; those who believed Peter's testimony; also believed the truth of Jesus Christ and that He was raised from the dead and exalted by God; and that they needed to repent of their rebellion against God. Then these new disciples were baptized.

The number of new disciples that day, those added to the group of disciples, was about three thousand souls. In actual fact, it was probably much more than that because it is entirely likely that they only counted the men. Sadly, in that society, women and young people were not considered important enough to be counted for much at all and so the full number of converts could have been far greater than 3,000.

This is an incredible increase. From 120 followers of Jesus hiding in an upper room in Jerusalem, to thousands of believers who witnessed the disciples speaking in their own native tongues through the power of the Holy Spirit, who heard Peter's sermon about Jesus, and his call to repentance, and who then responded in obedience. All of this was done through and at the prompting of the Holy Spirit of God - the same Holy Spirit Who is available to us today.

We are called to go out in the power of the same Holy Spirit and proclaim the message the Spirit gives us. Yes, we have access to the same Spirit of God we see poured out the day the church was born. So, there is no reason why what happened on Pentecost cannot right here, today!

It is the Holy Spirit's doing.
It is the Holy Spirit Who does the convicting.
It is the Holy Spirit Who gives the understanding.
It is the Holy Spirit Who provides the confidence.
It is the Holy Spirit Who provides the message.

The only question we need to answer is, are we willing vessels or conduits of the Spirit?

What happened at Pentecost that day can happen today! There is no reason why it shouldn't be happening right now. Every church building should be full to overflowing. We all love this incredible story in Acts 2 of the birth of the church. What an amazing day that was. What an awesome sermon from Peter. What an outstanding outcome with so many coming to Christ.

The problem is, most of us treat this narrative like a fairy tale or a snapshot of an event so far removed from us today that the best we can do is imagine being there that day. Instead, we should be imagining that day being here! Why is it easier to imagine that we are observers on that great day than to imagine that day being replicated here and now in our very midst?

All the ingredients for another Pentecostal awakening are still in place – they always have been! The world is a complete mess and in desperate need of Jesus. The disciples of Jesus are still here, ready and able to wait and pray and believe like the disciples did in that upper room and at the temple for ten days.

The Holy Spirit Who was responsible for that whole remarkable event, is the same Holy Spirit Who inhabits God's people and longs to revive the church He birthed all those years ago. What is missing? We know the answer, don't we? We just don't want to say it out loud or admit it.

The only thing that is missing is our faith and our belief that God can and will do today what He did on the day the church was born, and our willingness to step out like Peter and the other Apostles did and become available to the Holy Spirit to bring the same community-wide transformation He did at the beginning.

I pray that as we journey through the book of Acts and start to re-connect with our spiritual roots, that God will open our eyes and our hearts as we accept His call once again to embrace the mission of Christ fully.

CHAPTER NINE
Devoted or Disinterested?

The members of Parker Memorial Baptist church in Silver Spring Maryland (USA) had an amazing vision: The saw a new Worship Centre seating 1,500 people rising in a former cornfield they had purchased at a bargain price. Residents of nearby homes had a different vision: hundreds of cars clogging their narrow, once quiet and peaceful street. They opposed the Church's plans and the local Council rejected their Development Application.

Churches were once considered community assets. But across America, UK and Australia, houses of worship now are joining chemical plants and landfills as frequent targets of the NIMBY syndrome. Do you know what that stands for? *Not in my back yard!* There is no doubt that churches are experiencing much less acceptance in our communities today. Our society has changed a lot over the last fifty years. The Christian church used to be regarded as not only a legitimate but a necessary part of every community. No longer. Today's culture is far too pluralistic for that. Now you may want to debate the merits or flaws in the current direction of our society, so let's just focus on the church.

While there is no doubt that churches are not being treated with as much respect as they once were, we should note that the early church, after it became strong, was violently opposed by many. It became a threat to the whole society as they knew it and it was not welcomed at all. Rather than being considered a community asset, the church was considered counter-cultural because it stood for a standard of righteousness the community simply did not desire or pursue and more.

Perhaps we should be upset in the church when we are not opposed for our bold stand for righteousness. It could be because either we do not stand for the right things or that our stand is not made known. Jesus warned us when He said, "*Woe to you when all men speak well of you*" (Luke 6:26). The character of a person is known not only by his friends but also by his enemies.

However, in spite of the animosity which was directed towards the early church, it grew at a breathtaking pace and had a huge impact on the society around it. Why is that? What made the early church stand out from its culture?

We have already seen how the early church got its start with an amazing encounter with the living God on the Day of Pentecost. Thousands were brought to faith in Christ that day and were added to the church there in Jerusalem. But their faith not only changed their destiny, it also changed their lives.

As I am sure you already know, what you believe - affects how you live. This was certainly true for the first church. Their lives were transformed by this encounter with God. Their priorities suddenly changed. Think about it. They had come to Jerusalem for the great feast. They had taken this time out of their lives for this religious observance, but they were not just a bunch of homeless, jobless people with nothing else to do. They were ordinary people with families to support, work to pursue etc. However, all that changed for them.

Before this momentous transformation, they may have been focused on their jobs, their social relationships, their recreation and a host of other things. Now they were focused on Jesus Christ and His church. Their behaviour changed to reflect their new priorities. They made time for the things that were important to them.

We all do this. Generally speaking, the maxim is true which says, *People do what they want to do.* When your priorities change, your behaviour changes to reflect your new priorities. What you are passionate about, directly impacts how you live. That was certainly true for the early Christians.

> *"They devoted themselves to the apostles' teaching and to fellowship, to the breaking of bread and to prayer."* (Acts 2:42)

The NASB translation reads, *'continually devoting themselves.'* Literally, it reads that they were continuing steadfastly.

Here we have people who came to faith in Christ in a miraculous revival meeting one day during Pentecost. Yet, what happened to them completely transformed their lives. It transformed their behaviour. It is as if they understood that they would never be the same. And so, they began to live out that commitment in a very practical way every day. We see from this that a great church is a devoted church.

To what were these new disciples devoted? What were the things that this brand-new body of believers found important enough to commit themselves to? There are four mentioned in this one verse and for ease of memory I have used some alliteration. They were marked by a commitment to the truth, the tie, the table, and the throne.

1. The Truth: The Apostles' Teaching

They devoted themselves first to the Apostles' teaching. In other words, they gave a very high priority to understanding the truth. Now that they had come to faith in Jesus, they wanted to know more about Him. They wanted to understand how to apply His teaching to their lives. And so, they continually met together to hear the Apostles teaching, steadfastly devoting themselves to hearing, understanding and personally applying the teaching of the Apostles.

Devotion to knowing the truth was not only important in the early church, but it is sorely needed in the church today. In fact, we are seeing everywhere the fruits of <u>not</u> knowing the truth of God's word. The level of theological literacy among believers is, I believe, at its lowest ebb since the church was born. Thinking Biblically about the world around us should come naturally for devoted disciples, but it doesn't for most today. The issues that dominate our culture are the issues with which the church must grapple. Do we have answers to the questions people are asking? I don't mean pat answers, full of cliches and simple solutions, but answers that have substance and which are grounded in God's truth? Have we learned to think Biblically about the issues we face today in our contemporary culture?

- 84 -

What do we say about the moral decay in our society? What do say about the political forces at work and how they are shaping our society? What do we say about the scientific 'truth' which bombards us every day and impacts our lives more and more? Is that 'truth' consistent with the Truth God has given us? What do we do when it is not?

Unless we clearly know what the Bible says concerning these issues, we will not have any real answers for others or even for ourselves. We also need to know what the Bible says about the church, otherwise the whole community which Jesus birthed and promised to build can be led astray and, sadly, has been led astray in so many places in our world today.

It is tragic that even Christians, who should know the Scriptures, who should really know the Truth, are being led astray by so much false teaching concerning Christianity. Many Christians do not even know how to test these teachings to see if they are right, and as a result, we are now hearing and reading the strangest things coming from believers who have been completely duped by false teaching.

We must learn to be more like the Bereans, whom the Bible says, *"examined the Scriptures every day to see if what Paul said was true."* (Acts 17:11)

We all need to remember that everything should be tested by Scripture and ultimately, by the Holy Spirit. Therefore, we must have more than just a superficial knowledge of the Truth in the Scriptures and the Truth which the Holy Spirit brings to us.

Are you devoted to the apostles' teaching? In our day, that is essentially the New Testament. How devoted are you today to the teaching of the New Testament about Christ, the church, the world, your salvation and your purpose in this world?

This truth is readily available to us every day and it is taught each week in Biblical church fellowships. The question remains: how devoted are we to this Truth?

2. The Tie: Fellowship

Do you remember John Fawcett's old hymn which begins,

> *Blest be the tie that binds, our hearts in Christian love*
> *the fellowship of kindred minds, is like to that above.*

The tie that binds is the second thing the early believers devoted themselves to, and that was fellowship. It is interesting to me how so many people think they really don't need the fellowship of other believers. This was certainly not the case for the believers in the early church. They affirmed the need to continually devote themselves to a shared life with the other believers. In fact, they were together every day – not just once a week.

This is the tie that binds our hearts in love. The fellowship to which they devoted themselves was both the community of believers in the local church and the relationships of love made possible by that community. We can see both *"the fellowship"* (assembling together with the church) and *"fellowship"* (sharing common life in Christ) in view here. The writer to the Hebrews admonishes us strongly when he writes:

> *"Let us not give up meeting together, as some are in the habit of doing, but let us encourage one another - and all the more as you see the Day approaching." (Hebrews 10:25)*

Here we can find the essence of what the first church captured in their devotion to the fellowship. You can only experience true fellowship by giving diligent attention to meeting together with those in the fellowship. The former is dependent on the latter. If you absent yourself from meeting together with other believers here, you will obviously not enjoy fellowship with them, and you should not be surprised at this.

It takes time and effort to develop meaningful relationships with others, even in the church. Why should that be different? In fact, it may even be a little more difficult in the church because we are called to develop relationships with people who are not 'like us' and with whom we might not naturally share fellowship.

People generally gravitate to others who like them in some way. We find people who are our same age, or have a similar situation in life, like small children, or no children. We find people who share our interests. But in the church, where God arranges the parts of the Body (1 Corinthians 12:18), we are put together with many others who are not like us. In the Christian church, our common interest is Christ and so we are to transcend issues like age, education, social status, situation in life, race, and the like. This is the beauty and the mystery of the church, and a testimony to the world of the unifying love of Christ.

3. The Table: Breaking of Bread

They also devoted themselves to the breaking of bread. Now this could mean one of two things, or perhaps both. It could mean that they shared their meals together. Or it could mean that they devoted themselves to the ordinance of the Lord's Supper or Communion as many people call it. Perhaps both are involved.

Because they had been gathered together into this one fellowship by the sacrifice of Jesus Christ, these newly baptised believers began to celebrate their unity with and love for one another, and their worship and reverence for Christ. One way they did that was to share meals together. Another way they 'broke bread' together was to celebrate Communion. Or perhaps it was both at the same time?

A number of historians support this view. There is evidence to suggest that the early Christians celebrated the Communion as a part of a shared meal. Like any close-knit church, they would eat together frequently, perhaps a lot more frequently than most churches do today. At the very least they would probably share a meal following each Lord's Day service. This would not be unusual for their culture. Many cultures today also do this. I know that many of our Filipino and Korean brothers and sisters do. In any case, their celebration of the Communion took on a different form than ours. It was not the sombre, almost funeral-like event that you still see in many places today. It was reverent - but joyful, prayerful - but full of rejoicing.

Although the Scriptures do not give us specific details as to how we are to share this special time together, other than to remember Christ's death when we do it, we should learn something from these early Christians about how to observe this aspect of our faith – especially noting the importance they placed on it.

4. The Throne: Prayer

Finally, it says that they devoted themselves to prayer. Their focus was heavenward, toward the throne. Their focus was on God Himself. So, they gave themselves to a life of prayer. Jesus said that His house should be known as a "house of prayer." This early church knew the necessity of seeking God and His will in prayer. They knew that it took a continual, daily devotion to prayer. A great church must be a praying church. A great church will devote itself to prayer because we depend upon God for our existence and certainly His wisdom and direction in ministry.

Unfortunately, over the last hundred years, prayer seems to have become a dying art among Christians. Many believers affirm that they believe in prayer, but few people really spend much time praying. Of course, almost everyone sends up a brief prayer from time to time, some may even send up several a day. But how many believers today spend significant time in prayer?

Fewer still spend any time in communal prayer – that is prayer with other believers. Have you noticed the death of the church prayer meeting? It seemed to die years ago in most churches. Announce a fellowship lunch and you will probably have a full house. Announce a prayer meeting and you may be there alone. I am sure there are some churches today that call one of their services a prayer meeting, but it's usually only another meeting for Bible study and worship. Prayers may be offered, but it is not a meeting which is devoted to prayer.

Of course, one of the reasons for this is that many people do not want to pray in a group of people. They are actually embarrassed to pray with others. Or they do not think that they would know what to say or how to say it. The real problem may be that they have not been taught how to pray.

Jesus' disciples felt this need profoundly and asked Jesus to teach them how to pray. They saw Jesus spend entire nights in prayer and they also saw the effect of that prayer. If we want to see the effect of prayer, we must pray! When we speak to others of our needs, we get whatever people can do. When we speak to God about our needs, we get whatever God can do! That's why James reminded us:

> "The prayer of a righteous man is powerful and effective."
> (James 5:16)

The reason for the power of prayer is that it engages God in the in our life and ministry. The early church quickly learned to use prayer effectively because they began to be persecuted. Peter and John were rebuked by the Sanhedrin. When they returned to the assembly, prayer was the first order of the day. Later, when Peter was imprisoned, the church came together to pray. The early church was devoted to prayer as a way of life and God moved in their midst as a result.

> "For though we live in the world, we do not wage war as the world does. The weapons we fight with are not the weapons of the world. On the contrary, they have divine power to demolish strongholds. We demolish arguments and every pretension that sets itself up against the knowledge of God, and we take captive every thought to make it obedient to Christ." (2 Corinthians 10:3-5)

> "For our struggle is not against flesh and blood, but against the rulers, against the authorities, against the powers of this dark world and against the spiritual forces of evil in the heavenly realms." (Ephesians 6:12)

Like it or not, we are engaged in a spiritual battle which must be won on our knees in prayer. For that to happen, we really must be devoted to prayer. Whether it happens in a designated prayer meeting, or one-on-one over coffee, or in our small groups or on a 'prayer walk' around our town with a brother or sister - our prayer ministry will take root and grow if and when we devote ourselves to prayer like the early church did.

A great church is a church in which people exhibit a deep level of commitment in their Christian walk - a clear devotion to the disciplines of the Christian faith. We must never forget that the call of Christ is a call to follow Him. It is not a call to subscribe intellectually to a set of religious teachings.

A great church is a devoted church, one in which people follow Jesus. It is a church where people live out the reality of New Testament Christianity, not merely a place where they only speak of it and sing about it. With such devotion, the giant will remain sleeping.

CHAPTER TEN
Koinonia Fellowship

In this book we have been exploring what it looks like to really *be* the church as it was in beginning and was always meant to be. This requires some study and serious reflection because the church which we have experienced for many generations now is radically different to the church which Jesus established. So, if we truly want to view the church from Jesus' perspective, we have to look beyond the corrupted visible church we have all inherited from our forebears.

Now you might think 'corrupted' is too strong a word, but I wish I had an even stronger word to describe how a dynamic, Spirit-led, Christ-centred, relational community could be transformed so radically into what is, more often than not, an event-based, task-centred, rule-governed religion.

Or in other cases the church has been reduced to a socio-political welfare agency with little or no reference to Christ or the gospel. You simply cannot look seriously at the early church and the modern church without scratching your head and wondering what on earth happened.

Let me give you a snapshot again of how it was when all of this began in this thing we call 'church' - to which we all profess to belong. I want you to imagine what this was like; how it worked; where it happened; how it felt; what impact it had on the people who were part of this miracle and the people watching on in the community around them.

You've read and heard this passage many times, but please don't allow familiarity to rob you of the impact of what is actually happening to and through these first believers, our pioneers, our ancient brothers and sisters in Christ.

As promised by Jesus Himself, the Holy Spirit came on the day of Pentecost and things got very messy, very exciting and very real - and here is the result.

Peter got up and told everybody what was really happening and how this was all part of God's plan and that this was exactly what Jesus came to create – a new community of faith, a new covenant of love and grace – and thousands of people said, *"Yes, please! Count me in!"* Then this new thing we call the church, began to take shape as ...

> *"... They devoted themselves to the apostles' teaching and to fellowship, to the breaking of bread and to prayer. Everyone was filled with awe at the many wonders and signs performed by the apostles. All the believers were together and had everything in common. They sold property and possessions to give to anyone who had need. Every day they continued to meet together in the temple courts. They broke bread in their homes and ate together with glad and sincere hearts, praising God and enjoying the favour of all the people. And the Lord added to their number daily those who were being saved."* (Acts 2:42-47)

I've read that passage thousands of times, and still it makes the hairs on the back of my neck stand up, as I anticipate what that must have been like. Each time I read those words, I also dream of the day when it will be like that again – a day when religion is finally sent back to the hell it came from and the community of faith which Jesus died to establish re-emerges in our midst with Jesus and His mission front and centre!

In the last chapter we were thinking about our devotion to the Apostles' teaching, which for us is the New Testament, and how important it was for us to connect with all that Jesus did and taught and then passed on to the Apostles. In this chapter I want to explore a much more challenging devotion – one which takes a lifetime to do well – one which so defined this new community.

I am talking about their devotion to fellowship. The Greek word translated as fellowship is *koinonia* and Acts 2 is the first time we encounter this word in the New Testament. In our context, this word 'fellowship' has been used beyond the confines of the church – but it shouldn't have been. This word is a Christian word because this fellowship is the unique fellowship we have together in Christ.

This is far more than a casual association or club membership or just having your name on a church roll. *Koinonia* fellowship is God-ordained, Christ-centred and Spirit-led. It only exists where the church exists and it speaks to the heart of this new movement which began over 2,000 years ago.

This radical concept of fellowship and interdependence flies in the face of the individualism which dominates our society and that only highlights our need to re-connect with the true nature of the church.

For millions of Christians today across the world, church life consists of a Sunday worship service and that's all - and even for those involved in a small group of some kind, the true purpose and importance of that small group is not fully understood by many.

Now I firmly believe in the tremendous value of communal celebration and worship on Sunday, or any day, and I believe that solid teaching times are crucial for our spiritual depth and strength. But you simply cannot read the New Testament and come away thinking that group gatherings in an auditorium once a week are the sum total of what church is supposed to be!

In fact, such gatherings, which have been the primary expression of the Christian church across much of the world for generations now, cannot be found in their current form anywhere in the New Testament – which is that foundational document upon which the church supposedly stands!

We have also recently endured a global pandemic which shut down those weekly face to face gatherings completely for many months and yet the church which Jesus promised to build didn't cease to exist.

Therefore, let's look more closely now at this wonderful concept, captured by the Greek word *koinonia*. This word appears 19 times in the New Testament and this is the first time. It literally means 'common' or 'communal' and it signifies a close relationship, a sharing together, a participation, an intimacy.

Now the word *koinonia* may only appear once in the passage I read from Acts 2, but the concept of koinonia runs through almost every sentence of this wonderful description of the church.

> *"They devoted themselves ... to fellowship [koinonia] .. All the believers were together [koinonia] and had everything in common. [koinonia] Every day they continued to meet together [koinonia]... They broke bread in their homes [koinonia] and ate together [koinonia] with glad and sincere hearts ..."*

At the very heart of this new community of faith was *koinonia* – rich, personal, intimate, daily fellowship. So, what brought them together in this close bond of fellowship? It wasn't sport, music, hobbies, race, gender, jobs, economics, education, personalities, or social status – no, nothing in this world created that special 'togetherness.' *Koinonia* is a Kingdom reality.

What brought them together was their shared life in Jesus Christ! This fellowship wasn't merely a social activity, shooting the breeze or hanging out together. Not that there's anything wrong with that, and that is often the starting point of true *koinonia* fellowship, but we need to realise that just socialising isn't what the Bible portrays as fellowship.

Fellowship also isn't a place or a description of a group. We can call our Congregation a 'Christian Fellowship' but that doesn't guarantee that *koinonia* is actually taking place. It's more than a place and it's more than an event. Fellowship is our common, shared life in Jesus Christ. Fellowship is never just a label – it's an experience.

> *"We proclaim to you what we have seen and heard, so that you also may have fellowship with us. And our fellowship is with the Father and with his Son, Jesus Christ." (1 John 1:3)*

Any gathering of the church that leaves Jesus out is not *koinonia*, it's not true fellowship. For something to qualify as Biblical fellowship, the manifest presence of Christ has to be evident.

True fellowship always begins with God. In the book of Acts they were called 'believers.' The glue that brings us together, holds us together, and keeps us together is Jesus Christ and our faith and belief in Him and His finished work of salvation. Look at what the Apostle Paul says about what happened to you when your eyes were opened to the reality of your Salvation in Christ.

> *"Consequently, you are no longer foreigners and aliens, but fellow citizens with God's people and members of God's household, built on the foundation of the apostles and prophets, with Christ Jesus himself as the chief cornerstone. In him the whole building is joined together and rises to become a holy temple in the Lord. And in him you too are being built together to become a dwelling in which God lives by his Spirit."*
> *(Ephesians 2:19-22)*

When we become believers, our eyes are opened to the union we have with Jesus Christ, we recognise that we are part of God's family and as such, we become aware of a whole household of brothers and sisters. When we have fellowship with Jesus Christ, the dynamic of that relationship is meant to outflow into many relationships – into fellowship with each other.

> *"If we walk in the light, as He is in the light, we have fellowship one with another."* *(1 John 1:7)*

So, in this modern era, is it even possible to experience this close, caring community like we see in the early church? What keeps this passage in Acts 2 from being a fairy tale from a lost era - an idealistic dream, rather than a 21st century reality? Can such a group of imperfect, forgiven believers really live together in community and intimacy? The Bible says we can.

God has designed us for closeness in the church Jesus promised to build and He wants us to make every effort to <u>be together</u> as often as we can. Being together is God's way of building *koinonia* in practical, visible, and tangible ways in the church. The New Testament stresses our involvement in this 'together' dynamic with a key truth captured in the recurring phrase 'one another'.

Just in case we miss the importance of fellowship and relating to each other, there are over thirty-five 'one another' statements in the New Testament. As you read them, don't let them just be 'theology' or 'doctrine' or a dry list in a book. I really want you to imagine what these concepts could actually look like and feel like in your life and in the lives of those around you who claim to be your brothers and sisters in Christ.

I want you to dream about the kind of church we will be when these statements are actually observations of who we are – rather than who we might like to be. Here are just some of the 'one another' statements from the Bible:

- Fellowship with one another (1 John 1:5-7)
- Confess your sins to one another (James 5:16)
- Offer hospitality to one another (1 Peter 4:9)
- Clothe yourselves with humility toward one another (1 Peter 5:5)
- Do not lie to one another (Colossians 3:9)
- Comfort and encourage one another (1 Thess. 4:18; 5:1)
- Spur one another to good deeds (Hebrews 10:24)
- Do not slander one another (James 4:1)
- Do not grumble at one another (James 5:9)
- Agree with one another (1 Corinthians 1:10)
- Serve one another (1 Corinthians 9:19 - 2 Corinthians 4:5)
- Have equal concern for one another (1 Corinthians 12:25)
- Do not be conceited, provoking and envying one another (Galatians 5:26)
- Restore one another (Galatians 6:1)
- Bear with one another (Ephesians 4:2 - Colossians 3:13)
- Be kind to one another (Ephesians 4:32)
- Sing to one another (Ephesians 5:19-20)
- Submit to one another (Ephesians 5:21)
- Wash one another's feet (John 13:14)

- Live in peace with one another (Romans 12:16)
- Honour one another (Romans 12:10 - Philippians 2:3)
- Stop judging one another (Romans 14:13)
- Accept one another (Romans 15:7)
- Teach and admonish one another (Colossians 3:16)
- Greet one another with a holy kiss (Romans 16:16)
- Love one another (John 13:34-35)

Now, let me ask you something: Can all these 'one anothers' happen in just one worship service every week? Of course they can't. That list itself demands a community of faith which shares its life together, just as they did when our church was born!

Sunday worship gatherings have a purpose. This is where we gather together in celebration and community worship and also receive teaching and celebrate communion and share fellowship. It is certainly not meant to be the only thing that happens each week for those who belong to the family of God. Being part of the church Jesus promised to build, consists of so much more than one weekly get-together.

Just imagine if we had only spent an hour or two once a week with our own families all those years we were together. What kind of relationship would we have with each other? How close would we be? How united in purpose would we be? How loved and appreciated and encouraged would we feel? How much would we be able to give to one another? How much would we even know each other? Well, so it is with the family of God – the community of faith – the church. Without the willingness to be involved in the lives of others, neither you nor they will grow and become the wondrous miracle the church was when it was born and is meant to still be today.

Ok, that's the easy part! Essential as it is to identify the need (some don't even bother doing that), the hard part is addressing that need by making different choices to the ones we've made in the past.

That's the only way things ever change. That's the only way the dynamic reality of the early church can be re-captured today – by people making different choices. Those choices could be as simple as deciding to invite someone from your church to your place for a meal to get to know them and their story and grow closer to them in their spiritual journey in Christ. Then invite someone different next time. Maybe make it a monthly thing. How hard could that be? Even just a phone call to catch up with someone from church and see how they are going can make a huge difference in their lives. It is not difficult to maintain fellowship, but it does require a commitment or it just won't happen.

Let me suggest that if everyone in every congregation decided to spend quality *koinonia* time together by phone or in person where possible, the Spirit of God would move through the church in like a raging fire! If hosting a meal is too much for you, then a cup of tea and a biscuit for morning or afternoon tea is more than enough reason to gather together and give God an opportunity to show you what *koinonia* fellowship really feels like! You could even meet downtown for a cuppa at a local café if you are not comfortable hosting people in your home.

One of the best vehicles for developing strong fellowship bonds within the church is the ministry of small groups. This is where we meet regularly with some of our brothers and sisters and study and unpack the Scriptures and share our lives together - learning from God through each other and the Bible. Every church which is thriving has a vibrant small group ministry.

There are many aspects to being part of the true church, but at the centre of them all – at the very heart of this organic, dynamic miracle of God, is *koinonia* – real fellowship: a dynamic, Spirit-led, gospel-centred, relational community.

From the moment the church was born, we have been presented with a choice every day of our lives: relationship or religion. Every morning as you begin a brand-new day, you have that same choice before you: relationship or religion.

Our relationship with God and with each other is what defines us as His people, His disciples, His church and if those relationships are growing, deepening and strengthening, then so too will the church. God guarantees it.

Do we want our church to impact the community around us? Do we want to see God adding to our number daily like He did when all this began? Some people should answer no, to be honest, because some people are comfortable with church as it is, as they have experienced it for many years. But those who answer yes and genuinely want to see the church at its best, must face the challenge God is presenting to us today, and every day.

If we want a different outcome,
we need to make different choices.

There is nothing very spiritual about that truth, that's just how life works on all levels. However, when you apply that statement to spiritual matters like the spread of the gospel and the health and growth of the church, the outcome will be life changing as the community around us is transformed by the power of God.

How devoted are we to *koinonia* fellowship, the community of faith which Jesus promised to build, not the institution which man has built in Jesus' name? May God help us answer that question in the days ahead and may we have the courage to make some different choices and thereby become the answers to our own prayers for our community and our nation.

Perhaps one of the greatest lessons we should have learned from the recent global pandemic is just how important fellowship is to the life and health of the church and the mission of Christ. It was really important to our pioneers in Acts 2, which is why it says, " ... *every day they met together.*" Why do we keep searching for the secret to church growth and church health when it has been staring us in the face for 2,000 years: " ... *every day they met together.*" May those who have ears to hear, listen to what the Spirit is saying to us today.

CHAPTER ELEVEN

Awesome!

"Everyone was filled with awe at the many wonders and signs performed by the Apostles." (Acts 2:43)

The way we use words is interesting, to say the least. In each generation, there has always been a lingo that has been used to express the feelings of a particular group. Terms like HIP, COOL, FAR OUT, OUT OF SIGHT, RAD, GROOVY and others like them have all been used at one time or another. Today, things seem to be changing so fast that it's really hard to keep up with the latest slang.

There are probably many reasons why a group adopts a certain set of words for its own use, but one reason is that they want to express a common understanding or feeling quickly. All these words serve as a code, a kind of short cut of expression. And people who are part of the 'in' group that uses these expressions know exactly what they mean.

The word AWESOME has been used a lot to express a certain feeling about something. To say something is awesome not only means it is something that inspires high appreciation but also reflects how we feel about it. And most of these words used that way are valuable because they communicate more than just facts. They communicate feelings - how we feel - and how we feel about things is important to us, sometimes even more important than what we think intellectually.

Feelings are important to us, more important than we often like to admit. Feelings can literally cripple us physically if they are strong enough. And the reason is that feelings affect our mind. If strong enough, feelings can overwhelm a person. On the other hand, feelings can impact us very positively as well. Feelings of confidence have been shown to be the difference in success and failure in the world's best athletics.

One person who is confident will succeed where another person of equal, and sometimes greater ability will fail because he or she lacked confidence. Our attitudes affect our relationship with God. Our attitudes do not change how God feels about us, but they do change how we feel about God. And how we feel about God will either enhance or impede our ability to trust Him and receive from Him.

What we see in the text above is a prime example of the kind of attitude that enables us to see and receive from God. This early church exemplifies the kind of response to God that we need in today's church.

> " … many wonders and miraculous signs were done by
> the Apostles."

One of the first things that jumps out at you, when you read this verse, is the miraculous - the signs and wonders done at the hands of the Apostles. For some reason we like to focus on these amazing displays of God's power. There is something within all of us that likes to be amazed.

When I watch some magic shows, I am spellbound by how the tricks are accomplished. But I think the real thrill is the surprise of seeing the unexpected happening right before my eyes. We are intrigued by the prospect of seeing signs and wonders. We would like for God to do a few for us.

In fact, some people try and turn God into some kind of cosmic magician to entertain us with His genuine magic show. This is what the religious leaders asked Jesus to do. It wasn't *"show me the money,"* it was *"show me a sign - show me a miracle."* But Jesus refused to be manipulated by their self-serving requests. He did perform miracles for the 'show.' He did them for a purpose. The same is true today.

This raises some questions: Why don't we see more signs and wonders today? Does God still perform signs and wonders? Is there something wrong with our ability to see them? Do we lack the faith necessary for God to work in our midst? What are the explanations for this?

Some people believe that wonders and miraculous signs passed away with the first apostles. They are known as cessationists, and these people teach that the miraculous gifts were given to authenticate the message being preached by these apostles and were not needed after that apostolic age passed.

You must remember that this was a brand-new message. There was no New Testament section of the Bible in those days. The New Testament as we have it today is the message of those first apostles. They were writing it.

So, how would people know that what they were saying is true? The answer the cessationist gives is that the miracles served this purpose – just for a time. During the birth and establishment of the early church the miracles functioned, and after it was established and the New Testament completed, the miracles ceased.

Now we are supposed to believe by faith in the authenticated word recorded on the pages of the New Testament. We don't need miracles.

Now this theory is partially true. It is true that miraculous signs were done in part to authenticate the preaching of the gospel. Paul alluded to this when he wrote:

> "*The things that mark an Apostle - signs, wonders and miracles – were done among you with great perseverance.*"
> (2 Corinthians 12:12)

There is no doubt that God worked in a special and unique way through these original apostles. They had, and will ever have, an honoured place in the Kingdom of God. But it's simply not true that signs and wonders by themselves are ever sufficient to authenticate a teaching.

> "*The coming of the lawless one will be in accordance with the work of Satan displayed in all kinds of counterfeit miracles, signs and wonders, and in every sort of evil that deceives those who are perishing.*" (2 Thessalonians 2:9-10)

There can certainly be counterfeit miracles as well. Now, they are counterfeit not because they are not miraculous but because they are done by the power of evil. Jesus told us that toward the end of time *"false Christs and false prophets will appear and perform great signs and miracles to deceive even the elect - if that were possible."* This theme is again emphasised in the book of Revelation, where it speaks of the deceiving power of the beast.

> *"And he performed great and miraculous signs, even causing fire to come down from heaven to earth in full view of men. Because of the signs he was given power to do on behalf of the first beast, he deceived the inhabitants of the earth."* (Revelation 13:13-14)

Signs and wonders in themselves can be the work of the enemy of God. They can be used by Satan to deceive people. So, we must beware. Even back in the Old Testament, God warned people:

> *"If a prophet, or one who foretells by dreams, appears among you and announces to you a miraculous sign or wonder, and if the sign or wonder of which he has spoken takes place, and he says, "Let us follow other gods" (gods you have not known) "and let us worship them," you must not listen to the words of that prophet or dreamer. The LORD your God is testing you to find out whether you love him with all your heart and with all your soul."* (Deuteronomy 13:1-3)

All things must be judged by whether they line up with the revealed word of God. This is the test for everything in the Christian life.

So, the miracles that were given to the apostles to do were not the sole verifying agent. They served an important purpose, but there is no reason to believe they were done simply to convince people. Paul, from whom we heard earlier about the signs of an apostle, explains it this way:

> *"Jews demand miraculous signs and Greeks look for wisdom, but we preach Christ crucified: a stumbling block to Jews and foolishness to Gentiles."* (1 Corinthians 1:22-23)

In other words, God will give faith to those who hear and receive the gospel. People will not believe simply because they see a miracle.

Another theory is that the reason we do not see more miracles today is because they never happened in the first place. Some have explained away miracles because they do not fit their view of the world. These people are rationalists and this is the view of what is known as theological liberalism.

Attempts have been made by liberals to demythologize the life of Jesus - to remove the miraculous elements from the story of His life, which they believe were added by zealous disciples embellishing the story as they retold it in later years.

But it seems to me that if you remove the miraculous, you lose any reason to believe that Jesus was more than any other teacher. You see, when you remove the miraculous or supernatural, you remove the literal resurrection, without which Paul says, "*And if Christ has not been raised, your faith is futile; you are still in your sins.*" (1 Corinthians 15:17). I have only one word to describe this view of theological liberalism - baloney!

Another view as to why we do not see more of the miraculous is because we do not understand God's ways. We see things from our limited perspective, not God's. Now, there is much to say for this view.

There are many examples from Scripture of how God's people missed what God was doing because of their limited vision and there is no doubt that God is up to more than we know. There is also no doubt that He does not perform simply because we want Him to thrill us. God never works to perform but to fulfil His purposes. We should not be surprised that we do not understand what He is doing at times, for His ways are higher than ours.

But there is yet another explanation that our text suggests.

"Everyone was filled with awe ..."

God was at work in this group of believers. They had been saved by His grace and were now devoting themselves to the apostles' teaching, fellowship, the breaking of bread, and to prayer. And their hearts were filled with awe.

Why were they filled with awe? Was it because of the miracles? Some would say it was, but perhaps that's not the only possible explanation. It could be that the miracles were done as a result of the atmosphere of faith which seemed to prevail in these awe-filled disciples.

Do you remember when Jesus visited to His hometown? When He arrived there, He encountered people who did not have faith in Him.

> "And He did not do many miracles there because of their lack of faith." (Matthew 13:58)

There seems to be a principle in God's Kingdom that God will withhold His miraculous power where there is no receptivity or where people's motives are wrong. I personally believe that this is one of the reasons why we do not see more happening in our Western culture. We have bought into this rationalistic way of thinking which suggests that everything can now be explained by science. We are simply not very open to the miraculous. We want to explain it away. Perhaps God will not cast His pearls before swine, so to speak?

One way this word *awe* can be translated is *fear*. To be filled with awe means that we are filled with a reverential fear before the presence of the Almighty. Some would say there is not enough of this in the church today. We truly worship an awesome God. We need to be more awestruck by His glorious, holy greatness. Now, by that I am not talking about the vacuous atmosphere of religious solemnity that still pervades many churches today. In some churches they have the idea that if you are able to create an atmosphere more like a funeral service, you are revering God. But this is not what being filled with holy fear means.

As a matter of fact, there have been times when people were so overcome by God's holiness and their lack of holiness, that they fell to the floor under the burden of their sin, loudly weeping and wailing; and times when people have become so overwhelmed with God's love and grace that they lay on the floor for hours just basking in his glory. This kind of thing was seen in New England during the Great Awakening under Jonathan Edwards. Being filled with awe can be very loud and somewhat messy!

Being filled with awe means that we have actually transcended our earthly view and have caught a glimpse of the eternal glory of the living God. It means that we have caught a vision of His greatness, His holiness, His power and His love. Like Isaiah in the temple, when we see the Lord high and lifted up, we fall at His feet in humble surrender and worship. This is the kind of atmosphere in which God begins to work in power. This is the kind of attitude we need in our lives today. This is the kind of attitude we need more of in our churches today. This was what the early Christians experienced as they began to follow Jesus and to share Him with others.

This also highlights an important truth we must try and grasp. God was at work through the people in order to bring people to Himself. These Christians were sharing with others and bringing people to Christ. Perhaps we do not see more of God because we are not doing what they were doing - we are not really sharing Jesus with anyone.

The sad truth is that there is a powerless Gospel being preached from many pulpits today. Jesus never intended that. To the contrary, the church that He established on this earth is called to preach the Gospel and to see the preaching of God's Word confirmed in Holy Spirit power, with supernatural signs and wonders following.

> *"After the Lord Jesus had spoken to them, he was taken up into heaven and he sat at the right hand of God. Then the disciples went out and preached everywhere, and the Lord worked with them and confirmed his word by the signs that accompanied it."* (Mark 16:19-20)

That is the pattern which Jesus gave to His church - we preach and teach His word throughout the world, and He faithfully confirms it with supernatural signs, healings, and miracles.

Sadly, however, many churches in our day are content with only preaching the word of God but have little or no expectation of supernatural gifts of the Spirit to confirm the word preached. This type of word-only ministry would have been completely foreign to the apostle Paul.

> "... because our gospel came to you not simply with words but also with power, with the Holy Spirit and deep conviction ..."
> (1 Thessalonians 1:5)

The manifestation of Holy Spirit power is absolutely essential to effective ministry as Jesus intended it. Signs and wonders will follow the preaching of the Word of God.

> " ... how shall we escape if we ignore so great a salvation? This salvation, which was first announced by the Lord, was confirmed to us by those who heard him. God also testified to it by signs, wonders and various miracles, and by gifts of the Holy Spirit distributed according to his will." (Hebrews 2:3-4)

Our job on earth is to announce to the world this great salvation that Jesus has provided for all who receive it. God's trustworthy promise is to testify to and confirm the Word with "...signs, wonders and various miracles, and by gifts of the Holy Spirit."

If you study the first ten spiritual awakenings or revivals in the Book of Acts, you will discover that nine of those ten were definitively linked to a notable sign, healing, or miracle.

Contrary to much that is practiced in churches today, after Jesus returned to heaven, the church that He founded continued to preach and teach the Word of the Lord with visible power. Not just power in their preaching, which of course we all desire, but also power to heal the sick, raise the dead, cleanse the lepers and cast out demons in Jesus' name, and more.

It was this combination of word-and-power that dramatically expanded the Kingdom of heaven on earth in the early years of the church.

> *"My message and my preaching were not with wise and persuasive words, but with a demonstration of the Spirit's power, so that your faith might not rest on human wisdom, but on God's power."* (1 Corinthians 2:4-5)

The truth stated in the above verses has motivated me strongly during my 40 plus years as a Spirit-led minister of the Gospel. I have exhorted many of my fellow preachers, not to be content with speaking "*wise and persuasive words ... [of] human wisdom*" from their pulpits – but to preach God's word and expect a faithful God to faithfully confirm His word "*by signs, wonders and various miracles, and by gifts of the Holy Spirit.*" (Hebrews 2:4).

So how about it then? Do we really have a zeal to share Jesus and expect God to confirm our words with signs and wonders? Have we become complacent in our Christianity? One of the greatest Christian songwriters, Keith Green, said it best when he sang: '*the world is lost in the darkness, while the church is asleep in the light.*'

I heard of a preacher many years ago who began a sermon by saying, "*The sad fact is that there are thousands of people around us in this very city who are lost in the darkness and most of you don't give a damn. And what is even sadder is that you will now be far more concerned that I said 'damn' than you are that these people are lost!*"

The Apostle Paul had more "*wise and persuasive words*" than any of his peers, but the reason revival followed him wherever he went was due to the demonstration of the Spirit's power, which always accompanied his words. We hear of many miraculous signs and wonders going on in parts of the world today where God's people are sharing Jesus and preaching the gospel - and many people are coming to Christ.

May God fill us with the holy awe that comes from seeing Him in all His glory, and may He reveal His miraculous power as we share Jesus with others!

CHAPTER TWELVE
A Giving church

The Sunday School Teacher asked her eight eager 10-year-olds if they would give $1,000,000 to the missionaries.

"*Yes!*" they all screamed!!

"*Would you give $1,000?*" Again, they shouted "*Yes!*"

"*How about $100?*"

"*Oh, YES we would!*" they all agreed!!

"*Would you give just a dollar to the missionaries?*" she asked.

The boys exclaimed "*Yes!*" just as before, except for Johnnie.

"*Johnnie,*" the teacher said as she noticed the boy clutching his pocket, "*why didn't you say 'Yes' this time?*"

"*Well,*" he stammered, "*because I have a dollar.*"

It has been said that money talks. The only problem is that for most of us these days it only says, "*Goodbye.*" But when you think about it, money does talk in many ways. It says a lot about the people who have it and those who seek to have it. Your attitude concerning money and the way you use your money says a great deal about you.

It might surprise you to find out that the Bible has quite a lot to say about money and possessions. In fact, there are well over a thousand references to money in the Bible, second only to the topic of love. More than half the parables Jesus told, of which we have a record, referred to money.

It should be obvious that our use of money always says volumes about us. It can say that we are greedy or generous, stingy or giving, corrupt or holy. It should be no surprise therefore, that the power of the Holy Spirit made a difference in how these early Christians dealt with money and material possessions.

When they came to Christ, they were utterly transformed in heart, mind, and lifestyle. That is what we see in the opening pages of the Book of Acts. We see people here who had been possessed by God. Here we see another mark of a great church - a church that is awake and alive and acting like it should. When the sleeping giant wakes up - we see a church that gives ... and gives generously.

> "They sold property and possessions to give to anyone who had need." (Acts 2:45)

These early Christians were so committed that some of them sold their possessions to help others in need. They seemed to be so overpowered by a spirit of generosity and giving that even their possessions were no longer as important to them. They were more concerned that in their church no one would suffer need. But what they provided was not merely spare change. It wasn't even a few thousand dollars sitting in the bank drawing interest. It was their houses, their land, and for some of them, all their possessions. What an unselfish spirit existed among these early Christians! They were a generous, giving church.

A truly great church will be a generous church. I don't believe God can do a lot with tight-fisted, materialistic, selfish, grasping, worldly Christians. That, at best, is carnal Christianity, and at worst, it's not Christianity at all. True Christianity is generous. True Christianity is giving.

"For God so loved the world that He gave..." God, in His very nature, is a giver. And we, if we contain the nature of God within our mortal flesh, will also be givers. A great church will always be a selfless church. Jesus told us that it is impossible to serve two masters - that we simply could not serve God and money at the same time. It is really a question of priorities.

He also told us that we should not be worried about even those basic needs that we all have - needs like food and clothing. The reason is clear. He has committed Himself to provide for our needs, and He wants us to trust in Him for those needs.

It is because we serve a God Who provides for us that we can give with the confidence that He will take care of us. This provides the motivation for sincere giving. Let's look at some characteristics which should mark generous Christian giving.

The first reason we ought to give is because we love the Lord and we are thankful for all God that has done for us. Remember, Jesus gave His very life for us. Considering what He gave, how small is the gift of a tithe? Small indeed. God has blessed us beyond what we deserve. Because of all He has done for us, we give out of a heart full of love for Him. We give because we want to - because we are thankful. So, our giving, first of all, should be thankful giving.

It is so easy to take things for granted. We live in a wonderful, free country. We are well fed. We have a roof over our heads, and money in our pockets. It's true, we might not be as well off as some, but compared to most of the world we are rich. We are not only blessed materially, but we are also blessed with friends, family, and a future. But, in spite of all this, we are sometimes slow to acknowledge our blessings. Because we have grown so accustomed to them, we can take them for granted. It's easy to do. Occasionally we need to be reminded of just what we have been taking for granted, and what we have to be thankful for. It is at special times, like birthdays and anniversaries that we are able to focus our attention on the things which really count.

What is the basis for true thanksgiving? Well, to be thankful, one must be grateful for something, and to someone. It has been said that *"The atheist's most embarrassing moment is when he feels profoundly thankful for something but can't think of anybody to thank for it."* The real basis for giving thanks is found in a Person.

The greatest gift ever given, by the greatest Person, was God's Son, Jesus. He's the real basis for all thanksgiving. The greatest gift that anyone has ever given to humankind is the gift of eternal life through Jesus Christ.

"Thanks be to God for His indescribable gift!" (2 Cor. 9:15)

This is what is called the Gospel. *Gospel* means *good news* and it is good news indeed! Those of us who have experienced the effects of this good news in our lives also know the gratitude we feel towards God. How can we ever thank Him enough? Human words fail to adequately express the overwhelming gratitude which wells up in our hearts.

The basis for true thanksgiving is an encounter with the living God. As we get to know Jesus better, we will find that our gratitude grows. We ought to give because of an attitude of gratitude.

Our giving also ought to be cheerful giving. The Bible tells us that *"God loves a cheerful giver."* (2 Corinthians 9:7). It has been said that while God loves a cheerful giver, He will take money from a scrooge. But that is not His desire.

The word for *cheerful* in 2 Corinthians 9:7 is the word from which we also get our word *hilarious*. God loves a giver who gives joyously, hilariously; not simply because we have to, but because we delight in giving. And that kind of giving always brings God's blessings.

Giving should be characterised by a certain euphoria. It should be a joy to give to God. Perhaps we should collect the offering in our church in a new way. Instead of passing around the plates, maybe the people can dance down the isles in hilarious laughter and give! Giving should be a celebration of the grace of God.

This kind of giving does something important in our lives. Richard J. Foster, in his book Money, Sex & Power says this:

> *"Giving with glad and generous hearts has a way of routing out the tough old miser within us. Even the poor need to know that they can give. Just the very act of letting go of money, or some other treasure, does something within us. It destroys the demon of greed."*

Our giving should also be liberal. No, I am not talking about politics, I am talking about the true meaning of 'liberal' which is generous, abundant, unrestrained etc.

"Give, and it will be given to you. A good measure, pressed down, shaken together and running over, will be poured into your lap. For with the measure you use, it will be measured to you."
(Luke 6:38)

"Remember this: whoever sows sparingly will also reap sparingly, and whoever sows generously will also reap generously."
(2 Corinthians 9:6)

If we are stingy with our sowing, we shall be sadly disappointed with our reaping. The measure we pour out shall impact the measure we get back. If we give stingily, we shall reap stingily. If we give bountifully, we shall receive in abundance. While you can't out-give God, many certainly under-give Him. It has been said that *"Some give their money as they give their teeth to a dentist."*

In fact, there is even a disease associated with a lack of giving which is particularly virulent in the 21st century. It is called *cirrhosis of the giver*. It was actually discovered about 34 AD and ran a terminal course in a couple named Ananias and Sapphira (Acts 5). It is an acute condition which renders the patient's hand immobile when it attempts to move from the wallet or purse to the offering plate or to a person in need.

However, it is clinically observable that this condition seems to completely disappear in alternate environments such as the golf course, music concerts or a good restaurant. This is not Christian giving. The Lord loves a liberal giver. Our giving, as was the giving of the early church, should also be sacrificial in nature.

"And now, brothers and sisters, we want you to know about the grace that God has given the Macedonian churches. In the midst of a very severe trial, their overflowing joy and their extreme poverty welled up in rich generosity.

For I testify that they gave as much as they were able, and even beyond their ability. Entirely on their own, they urgently pleaded with us for the privilege of sharing in this service to the Lord's people." (2 Corinthians 8:1-4)

They not only gave out of their excess; they gave out of their need. Most people give only out of their surplus. Jesus is not too impressed with that kind of giving. But He rejoices in the person who gives over and above the tithe, over and above what may be expected. The person who lives more simply so that the Lord's work can prosper is the one who stores up treasure in Heaven. We do not lose what we give. We send it on before us as we wait for our treasure in Heaven.

There is a direct relationship between giving now and the future. I heard of a very wealthy woman who lived in a palatial home, surrounded by fine tapestries, linens, imported china, expensive bric-a-brac, and who indulged in every luxury imaginable. She died and went to the gates of Heaven.

An angel was chosen to accompany her to her new home. They passed many homes of grandeur and magnificence. Finally, they came to this street of much less glamour, and down at the end of it was a very humble little cottage. They turned to enter, and the woman stopped and looked about with tragic disappointment on her face.

The angel said to her, *"This is to be your eternal home."*

"Oh but," she said, *"I have been accustomed only to the finest and most expensive. There are many, many beautiful homes which we passed similar to mine on earth. There must be some mistake."*

"Ah," said the angel, *"we built your eternal home here from what you sent ahead during your live on earth, and this is the best we could do."*

Now I don't accept the theology of that story – but it is meant to make us stop and think what it really means to *'store up treasures in heaven.'*

Many will be surprised at the linkage between giving and God's blessing. Many have been blessed even in this life by giving. J.L.Kraft, head of the Kraft Cheese Corporation, who had given approximately 25 percent of his enormous income to Christian causes for many years, once said this:

"The only investment I ever made which has paid constantly increasing dividends, is the money I have given to the Lord. Pastors will do their greatest service in leading their people to understand the truth of God concerning the stewardship of time and money."

John D. Rockefeller explained a great principle when he said:

"I never would have been able to tithe the first million dollars I ever made if I had not tithed my first salary, which was $1.50 a week."

Other examples include John Wanamaker of Philadelphia, who from the beginning of his business career is said to have dedicated one tenth of his increase to the Lord. Likewise, William Colgate, the great soap and perfume manufacturer, rose to fame and wealth while consistently paying a tithe of his earnings into the gospel treasury. For him, this was the absolute minimum requirement designated by divine wisdom; and year by year as God prospered his efforts and multiplied his wealth, Colgate gladly gave far more than a tenth.

Now we need to understand that this is not prosperity theology. This is not giving so that we get something back. This is simply the principle of sowing and reaping. This is cause and effect. This is a law of the Kingdom. This is the truth about giving.

The real question we must ask ourselves is, *"What does our giving say about us?"* And then we must ask, *"What do we want our giving to say about us?"* How you respond to those questions will in a large measure determine the blessing of God on both yourself and the church.

A great church is a generous church. A great church is a giving church. These early Christians gave because their lives had been changed and, as a result of their spirit of generosity, God blessed the whole church, and through the church, He blessed the whole world. Think about the selfish bent of our society today and what this kind of unselfish, future-looking giving says to our greedy, materialistic generation. Giving shows the world that we really believe in eternity. Only one who knows that this life is not all there is will truly give. When you think about it, generous giving tells the world that you really believe.

Tony Campolo once asked the question, *"Can a Christian drive a BMW?"* He asked it, of course, to get the attention of Christians who had swallowed the materialistic philosophy of the age. But perhaps we can ask another similar and equally blunt question. *"Can you be a true Christian and refuse to give?"* I think the answer would be the same as Campolo gave: no.

Chuck Swindoll, in his book *Improving Your Serve* tells this story:

Shortly after World War II came to an and, Europe began picking up the pieces. Much of the Old Country had been ravaged by war and was in ruins. Perhaps the saddest sight of all was that of little orphaned children starving in the streets of those war-torn cities. Early one chilly morning an American soldier was making his way back to the barracks in London.

As he turned the corner in his jeep, he spotted a little lad with his nose pressed to the window of a pastry shop. Inside the cook was kneading dough for a fresh batch of doughnuts. The hungry boy stared in silence, watching every move.

The soldier pulled his jeep over to the curb, stopped, got out and walked quietly over to where the little fellow was standing. Through the steamed-up window he could see all the mouth-watering morsels as they were being pulled out from the oven, piping hot.

The boy salivated and let out a slight groan as he watched the pastry chef place them ever so carefully onto the glass-enclosed counter. The soldier's heart went out to the nameless orphan as he stood beside him. *"Son ... would you like some of those?"* The boy was startled. *"Oh, yeah ... I surely would!"*

The American stepped inside and bought a dozen, put them in a bag, and walked back to where the lad was standing in the foggy cold of the London morning. He smiled, held out the bag, and said simply: *"Here you are."*

As he turned to walk away, he felt a tug on his coat. He looked back and heard the child ask quietly: *"Mister ... are you God?"*

We are never more like God than when we give. *"God so loved the world, that he gave..."* If we are spirit-filled Christians serving that same God, then we will also be those who give ... not just our spare change ... not just our surplus ... we will give far more than that and we will do it with thankful hearts; we will do it with joy; we will do it sacrificially and we will do it generously.

What's the biggest misconception Christians have about giving? That when we give money away to a church or ministry, or to help the needy, it's gone. While we hope others will benefit from it, we're quite sure we won't. We think we're divesting ourselves of money, disassociating from it. Once it leaves our hands, we imagine, it has no connection to us, no future implications relevant to our lives. We could not be more wrong!

What we think we own will be rudely taken from us - some of it before we die, and anything that's left the moment we die. But now we have a window of opportunity not to divest ourselves of money but to invest it in the Kingdom of heaven. We don't have to have everything taken from us. We can give it before disaster or death strike.

Now is our chance to give what we can't keep - to gain what we can't lose. We are God's money managers. He wants us to invest in his eternal Kingdom. He tells us He's keeping track of every cup of cold water we give the needy in His name. He promises us He will reward us in heaven because we help the poor and needy who cannot pay us back for what we do for them. We can pay it forward into God's kingdom. We can invest in eternity.

This is the secret the early church learned very quickly and their wonderful generosity stands as an indictment, but also a great encouragement and example to us today.

CHAPTER THIRTEEN

United We Stand

"All the believers were together and had everything in common."
(Acts 2:44)

Walking across a bridge one day, I saw a man standing on the edge, about to jump off. I immediately ran over and said:

"Stop! Don't do it!"

"Why shouldn't I?" he said.

"Well, there's so much to live for!" I said.

"Like what?"

"Well, are you religious or atheist?"

"Religious."

"Me too! Are you Christian or Jewish?"

"Christian."

"Me too! Are you Catholic or Protestant?"

"Protestant."

"Me too! Are you Presbyterian or Baptist?"

"Baptist."

"Wow! Me too! Are you Original Baptist church of God, or are you Reformed Baptist church of God?"

"Reformed Baptist church of God."

"Me too! Are you Reformed Baptist church of God, reformation of 1879, or Reformed Baptist church of God, reformation of 1915?"

"Reformed Baptist church of God, reformation of 1915!"

To which I said, "Die, heretic scum!" as I pushed him off.

When it comes to unity, it would be fair to say that the church has drifted a long way from the second chapter of Acts where all the believers were together and had everything in common.

My 'man on the bridge' story is pure fiction, of course, however it is confronting how closely it might reflect how far we have fallen from those early says of the church. What essentially began as one church, united in their new-found faith in Jesus Christ, soon began to split, fragment and tear itself apart in disputes, schisms and bitter divisions.

Fast forward to the present day and that single united group of dedicated disciples has now fragmented into more than 45,000 separate denominations – each one claiming to be followers of Christ and part of the church He birthed. There is now so much division and intolerance in the church. It seems that some people want others to agree on everything, and when others don't think like they do, they withdraw their fellowship and friendship and establish another group which will align with their position.

I once heard the President of a major Bible college in the USA say that a certain denomination was *"the most united denomination he had ever seen."* Of course, his tongue was firmly planted in his cheek as he went on to say that in this denomination there was a small group united over here, and another small group united over there, and another small group united somewhere else. He was actually highlighting the serious division, not the unity in that denomination.

So many times, churches split because of a lack of unity. I can remember one such church split where one group which broke away then had the hide to include the word 'united' in their new church name! Calling ourselves *united* does not equate to unity.

It has always been fascinating to me why so many cults and other misguided fringe groups have so much success. Some of these groups proclaim a message which is much harder to believe than biblical Christianity.

If one has to take a step of faith to believe the Christian message, then you need a launching pad and booster rocket to believe many of these cult messages! Yet they continue to grow and find considerable success. Why is that?

One factor is their commitment to hard work. Evangelism is not optional with them. It is central to their purpose for existing. While the same should be true for us, many Christians simply do not take personal evangelism seriously. Another reason, and I believe the main reason why these cults are so successful, is that they are uncompromisingly united. They have a shared vision, a common goal, a singular purpose - and they go after their goal with total, unwavering zeal. I believe that this is why they are so successful. Deceived and dangerous, yes, but completely united.

This kind of unity is very attractive to people – especially those who are weary of the religious confusion and uncertainty they have experienced in many main-line churches. Unity is so very important. God designed us to be united as a people and we will always be attracted to unity, even if it's not for a good cause.

The early church was definitely a united church. They exhibited a level of unity and oneness that will forever be an example and challenge to churches everywhere. Notice that it says that the believers were *together*. In Acts 2 there is a lot said about being *together*. At the very beginning of the chapter we read, *"When the day of Pentecost came, they were all together in one place."* Then in verse 46 we read, *"Every day they continued to meet together in the temple courts. They broke bread in their homes and ate together with glad and sincere hearts."* There is something about togetherness that is so foundational for unity. Coming together is the first step toward unity. In fact, it is so important that the very phrase *"come together"* has become a synonym for unity.

When God sets His people free in Christ, He draws them into a community called the local church. This simply means that He puts us together physically. He wants us to learn to love each other. He wants us to find a way to pull together in the same direction. This is what He did with those early disciples in the upper room. The 120 who were waiting for the power of the Holy Spirit to come upon them were together day and night in the upper room. What do you think they were doing all that time? Well, they were certainly praying a lot of the time. But they were also talking, sharing their lives, their fears, their hopes, their aspirations and hesitations.

They were taking time to develop relationships and to become one people. They were becoming a team, a community. This can only happen when we take the time to be together as a church. It only happens when we choose to be more than an occasional participant in the life of the church. This is a real problem for the church in today's society. Our western culture is now decidedly slanted against the church.

When I was younger, our culture not only accommodated the church, but it supported Christianity. Sundays were considered a day that was set-aside for God. There were laws in place which mandated the closing of places of business and most shops on Sundays.

In many places across the USA 'Bible belt' public schools gave no homework on Wednesdays because they knew churches had Wednesday evening Bible Studies or mid-week services. There was no sport on Sundays. The Christians would not stand for it.

In fact, apart from emergency services, hospitals and some petrol stations, the entire society would effectively shut down on Sundays because of the high level of support for the Christian church. Oh, how things have changed!

In today's world, everything has changed. In fact, Sunday is now the biggest sporting day of the week in our culture and often the most popular shopping day! The result is that now the level of involvement by Christians in the life of the church has markedly decreased.

In some churches you have to give an announcement three weeks in a row for everyone to hear it, because a third of the people are there one week, a third the next, and a third the next. No wonder we struggle to get any momentum in ministry!

As Christians now living in a counter-Christian or anti-Christian culture, we are going to have to make some serious choices concerning what we stand for and what we are committed to. We need to do it and the world needs to see us do it. We have to make time to be together.

When I began my journey with God after my baptism over fifty years ago, Sunday was church day – all day! There was an all-age Sunday School before the morning service. Then we had the morning worship service which was very often followed by a fellowship lunch. Usually there were some small groups or choir practice or some other activity in the afternoon. Then at 7pm we would gather again for evening worship. For many churches this service had a youth focus. Then the highlight of the week for many of us back then was what we called 'after-church' which was a singalong and supper at someone's home.

So, it was common for many people to leave home for church at 8am in the morning and not return home until after 9pm in the evening. That's a lot of 'together' time and most of our church buildings were full back then! Fast forward fifty years and many churches struggle to get their people to commit to one hour on Sundays.

These first church believers in Acts 2 were so united that it says that they had everything in common. They saw themselves as one body of believers in Christ. It was not 'every man for himself' but rather, 'one for all and all for one.' They had not joined an organisation, they were joined together in an organism, a living, multi-membered body, of which Jesus is the head. They enjoyed genuine, God-ordained and God-empowered unity. This was not uniformity, where everyone believed the same thing, acted the same and lived the same. This was true spiritual unity which God empowers by His indwelling Spirit.

This kind of unity is something only God can bring but He can only create that miracle when His people make a conscious choice, every day, that they will come together, despite their differences. I'm sure there were differences in the early church.

After all, you will remember that these were Jews who came to know Christ and the Jews were notorious for their arguments and disagreements. How was it that this early church was so united? Well, I believe the answer lies in the fact that they knew that the church did not belong to them.

Jesus said, *"I will build My church ..."* (Matthew 16:18). He was and He is the head of the church. It is His will which is supreme. It is His will to which we defer. If we are to experience true unity, it must be around the will of God as manifested in and through Christ. It cannot be dependent upon our opinions or preferences. A great church is a united church, in Christ through Christ and for Christ.

Disunity can kill a church fellowship. It happens every day of the week somewhere in the world. In Paul's first letter to the Corinthians, he issues a powerful plea for unity in the local church. He finds it necessary to exhort the church in Corinth to be united and he admonishes them for their disunity.

> *"Now I exhort you, brethren, by the name of our Lord Jesus Christ, that you all agree, and there be no divisions among you, but you be made complete in the same mind and in the same judgment. For I have been informed concerning you, my brethren, by Chloe's people, that there are quarrels among you. Now I mean this, that each one of you is saying, "I am of Paul," and "I of Apollos," and "I of Cephas," and "I of Christ." (1 Cor. 1:10-12)*

This plea for unity was directed at the growing dissension in that church. We read of the quarrels which had emerged because the people were dividing into different factions, aligning themselves with various personalities. Four distinct camps were emerging. There was the camp of Paul, the camp of Apollos, the camp of Cephas, and the camp of Christ.

Both Paul and Apollos had ministered in Corinth. Undoubtedly a group of Jews in the church had been saved under Cephas. Apparently, people were attached to these gifted leaders and had a strong loyalty to them. Perhaps it was the content of their teaching or their style of ministry, but in any case, these three groups identified themselves by their teacher.

A fourth group had also arisen which seemed to think that they had a special claim on Christ. Perhaps they did not think they needed any human teacher.

Even though they used the name of Christ, they were still just as guilty of a party spirit as the other three groups. This was a real problem in the Corinthian church.

The source of their problem is also the source of most church conflicts today. It is a problem of selfishness. It is a problem of *"what I like,"* and of *"my opinion."* Look at what James says this:

> *"What is the source of quarrels and conflict among you? Is not the source your pleasures that wage war in your members?"* (James 4:1)

James identifies our own sinful, selfish desires as the source of quarrels and conflicts. And when you think of it, selfishness is really at the root of most sins. Selfishness never brings people together; it only drives them apart. But Christ's desire for us is that we become one. You will remember His prayer:

> *"I pray ... that all of them may be one, Father, just as you are in me and I am in you. May they also be in us so that the world may believe that you have sent me."* (John 17:20-21)

In light of the desire of Jesus, Paul issues this plea for unity. Paul pleads with them in the name of our Lord Jesus Christ that they come together and agree. He asks them to eliminate divisions, and to be made complete in the same mind and with the same judgment. This is a very powerful plea indeed. The phrase from the Greek, *"that you all agree"* translates literally as, *"that you all speak the same thing."* This is quite an amazing statement. Is it really possible for us to all speak the same thing? It becomes even more challenging when we read it from the Amplified Bible which attempts to give us the sense of the original language.

> *"But I urge and entreat you, brethren, by the name of our Lord Jesus Christ, that all of you be in perfect harmony, and full agreement in what you say, and that there be no dissensions or factions or divisions among you; but that you be perfectly united in your common understanding and in your opinions and judgments."*

Is it possible that we *"all speak the same thing?"* Can we really be *"perfectly united"* in our *"opinions"* and *"judgments?"* Surely it would be un-Australian for us all to have the same opinions. But this is precisely what Paul pleaded for. He called for no divisions.

The Greek word for *divisions* is *schismata*, from which we get the word *schism*. The figurative meaning is actually *"to tear or rip."* As applied in this passage, it means to have a serious difference of opinion, or a division of judgment. This was the kind of thing that Paul was arguing against. As Christians, our opinions ought to be subservient to Christ's opinion, and so we ought to be seeking to find out what is God's opinion and conform our opinions to His. It's simple really: we are all indwelt by the one Spirit, and when we submit to God's Spirit within us – unity is the guaranteed result. The Spirit of God cannot be divided.

Without this kind of unity, the mission of Christ is seriously impeded. Many young Christians have been confused and held back in their walk with God by supposedly mature believers who are propagating conflicting views about the Gospel, the Bible, and the central truths of our faith. This does not mean that we should uncritically accept one narrow body of doctrine. It does mean, however, that we must always give a clear and certain message when we speak concerning the truth of God. We must, for the sake of the Gospel, seek to speak the same thing. When we are together, we find that we are powerful.

In one of my favourite Peanuts cartoons, Lucy demands that Linus change TV channels and then she threatens him with her fist if he doesn't.

"What makes you think you can walk right in here and just take over?" asks Linus.

"These five fingers," says Lucy. *"Individually they're nothing but when I curl them together like this into a single unit, they form a weapon that is terrible to behold."*

"Which channel do you want?" asks Linus.

Turning away, he looks at his fingers and says, *"Why can't you guys get organised like that?"*

The kind of commonality we are talking about only comes as we embrace who we are in Christ and in His church. We must see that we are not only one with Christ, but we are also one with each other.

> *"For even as the body is one and yet has many members, and all the members of the body, though they are many, are one body, so also is Christ. For by one Spirit, we were all baptised into one body, whether Jews or Greeks, whether slaves or free, and we were all made to drink of one Spirit." (1 Corinthians 12:12-13)*

> *"We, who are many, are one body in Christ, and individually members of one another." (Romans 12:5)*

Let me say it again, the principle for unity in the local church is that we are one with Christ and one with each other. We must really grasp this truth. Remember that Jesus said that if we were one, the world would believe that the Father sent His Son (John 17:21). Unity among Christians testifies to the world that Jesus came because of the Father's love for them. Unity is essential in preaching the gospel. Unity is essential in carrying out this top priority of the church.

Here again we find a reason to come together, a cause to rally behind. When we begin to actively share the love of Jesus by sharing the good news of the gospel with others, we will find we are more united than ever before. This is our common task. When we give ourselves to it, we will see the hand of God empowering us and uniting us in Christ, through Christ and for Christ.

> *"And when they had prayed, the place where they had gathered together was shaken, and they were all filled with the Holy Spirit, and began to speak the word of God with boldness. And the congregation of those who believed were of one heart and soul." (Acts 4:31-32)*

Is that what you would like to see in your church and across your city? That is exactly what we will all see if we allow God to wake up the sleeping giant. When the church today makes the same commitment to unity the early church made, we will see the same result. It really is that simple!

CHAPTER FOURTEEN
Wake up and Worship!

John Bisagno told the story of being a Pastoral candidate for the First Baptist church in Houston. Back then it was a small church, located downtown. He said that when he walked in there were only a few people in a dimly lit sanctuary. The service was quite depressing. They were singing songs like funeral dirges.

Later that day John was walking around the downtown area and saw a jewellery store having a grand opening. He went in and it was bright and cheerful inside. There was upbeat and happy music playing. There were friendly and enthusiastic people who greeted him. They offered him some fruit punch to drink and showed him around the store. He remarked that if they had given an invitation, he would have joined the jewellery store, not the church.

Have you ever wondered why so many church services became so morbid at some point in our history? At what point in our history did we decide that when we come into a church building, we need to act in some religiously solemn way? Church, for so many, became more like a memorial service than a celebration. But it isn't a memorial service for the dead. Jesus did die, but He didn't stay dead! He is alive and supposedly present among us.

A church worship service should therefore not be like a funeral. Someone suggested that it's a memorial service, not *for* the dead, but *by* the dead! Perhaps that explains it. Thankfully this has changed in many churches over the past decade or two, but it is still a reality in so many places.

I think the primary reason most churches do what they do is because they have always done it that way. Most of us were brought up in churches that followed the traditions handed down by other churches, who followed the traditions handed down to them. Tradition has a great deal to do with why we do what we do and how the church functions today.

We are all creatures of habit. We've become accustomed to doing things the same way. All you have to do is think about your own personal ritual for getting up in the morning. Most people go through the same routine every day when they get up. Some switch the alarm clock off and lie there for just a few moments. Others sit on the side of the bed for a minute or two. Still others immediately spring forth to greet the new day. I'll bet you put your socks on the same way every morning. I'll bet that you put the same shoe on first every day. We all get into our routines. There's nothing wrong with that - it simplifies life somewhat and it makes us feel more comfortable.

There is nothing at all wrong with tradition. Some traditions are important. They can be valuable in communicating to us truth about God and about ourselves. One of my favourite musicals has been 'Fiddler on the Roof.' I particularly like the opening scene when Tevye sings the theme song, 'Tradition.' As he does, he explains to the audience the value of tradition as he sees it. He says, "*Our tradition tells us who God is and who we are.*" When tradition can do that, it is profoundly good.

Unfortunately, there are many traditions which are not Biblical traditions that permeate many churches today and tragically are thought of as essential. In fact, some things become almost holy and unchangeable. When those things are changed, people can become upset. It's as if we have somehow wilfully flaunted a commandment of the Lord when we tamper with these things. I have known people to be upset over where the piano is placed, where the preacher stands, even how the offering is collected. It is amazing the baggage we can build up in the church, and it doesn't take long to do it.

Our challenge is to always be faithful to the Bible. Baptists have been called 'People of the Book' because of our alleged stubborn determination not to have any other rule than the Bible to live by. Yet many times we are guilty of having tradition inform how we 'do church' more than the Bible. Think about this. If we did not have any tradition, no denominations, or anyone to tell us how to do things; if all we had was the Bible and the Holy Spirit, I wonder how church would look?

I know that we would do things differently. But that is the point! We should be doing things because we have been informed by the Bible rather than by traditions, however well-intentioned they may have been. In the early church we have a wonderful example of the way they came together as a church.

> *"Every day they continued to meet together in the temple courts. They broke bread in their homes and ate together with glad and sincere hearts, praising God and enjoying the favour of all the people." (Acts 2:46-47a)*

Notice the emphasis here on gladness and on praising God. Here is a joyously worshipping church. The mark of a great church is that it is a joyful church. It is a church which is characterised by praise. It is a worshipping church. Here are Christians who are gathering together for worship every day and wasn't drudgery. It wasn't ritualistic. They were coming together because they had experienced the joy of knowing Jesus Christ as Lord. These believers were excited about their relationship with God. Their services and their lives were characterised by praise. When people entered into their midst, they knew these people were excited and alive. No sour-faced Christianity to be seen. Here were people who clearly possessed the joy of knowing Jesus and that peace which passes all understanding.

It really does make a great difference when you come to a service in which people are excited, in which people are praising the Lord, where there is a real celebration of Christ's victory over sin and of His love for us. In the hymn we had at our wedding there is great line which says, "Let the Amen sound from His people again." When you are excited, it shows.

We really do have something to be excited about. We serve a Saviour Who loves us; a God Who has forgiven us; a Lord Who provides for our true needs; a Spirit Who empowers us. When you think of all that God has done for you, how can you not be excited? The only way I know not to be excited is either not to know Him, or to have drifted away from Him. And today, before you lie down to sleep tonight you can make sure that neither one of those situations is yours.

If you don't know Him, you can come to know Him today. And if you've drifted away from Him, you can return to Him today. Those of us who do know Jesus, ought to be a good example of enthusiasm in the church. Perhaps you know that the etymology of the word *enthusiasm* traces back to the Greek word *entheos*, which is a compound of *en* (meaning *in*) and *theos* (meaning *God*). So, true enthusiasm means that we are truly in God and God is in us. True enthusiasm, therefore, is simply how someone filled with the presence of God acts.

To be filled with God is to be filled with life, to be filled with love, to be filled with joy, to be filled with hope, to be filled with faith, to be filled with peace, to be filled with power. How would that make anyone feel and act? Well, they certainly would not act like they were in mourning! They would demonstrate and manifest the life that was within them.

This was true of the early church when they came together. Notice, it says that they had glad and sincere hearts, and that they were praising God. They were involved in joyous worship. So should our worship be. Of course, the worship of these early Christians was nothing new. They did not invent this. They were informed by another Biblical tradition, from what we call the Old Testament. It was the only Scriptures they had. Jewish worship was a celebration. They would sing, lift their hands, clap their hands, and even dance! This, of course has a great precedent in the Old Testament Scriptures. Here are just a few of the many examples:

> *"Sing joyfully to the LORD, you righteous; it is fitting for the upright to praise him. Praise the LORD with the harp; make music to him on the ten-stringed lyre. Sing to him a new song; play skilfully, and shout for joy." (Psalm 33:1-3)*

> *"Clap your hands, all you nations; shout to God with cries of joy." (Psalm 47:1)*

> *"Shout with joy to God, all the earth! Sing the glory of his name; make his praise glorious!" (Psalm 66:1-2)*

"My lips will shout for joy when I sing praise to you - I, whom you have redeemed." (Psalm 71:23)

"Come, let us sing for joy to the LORD; let us shout aloud to the Rock of our salvation. Let us come before him with thanksgiving and extol him with music and song." (Psalm 95:1-2)

"Shout for joy to the LORD, all the earth, burst into jubilant song with music; make music to the LORD with the harp, with the harp and the sound of singing, with trumpets and the blast of the ram's horn - shout for joy before the LORD, the King." (Psalm 98:4-6)

"Shout for joy to the LORD, all the earth. Worship the LORD with gladness; come before him with joyful songs. Know that the LORD is God. It is he who made us, and we are his; we are his people, the sheep of his pasture. Enter his gates with thanksgiving and his courts with praise; give thanks to him and praise his name. For the LORD is good and his love endures forever; his faithfulness continues through all generations." (Psalm 100)

"Let them praise his name with dancing and make music to him with tambourine and harp." (Psalm 149:3)

"Praise the Lord! Praise God in His sanctuary; Praise Him in His mighty expanse. Praise Him for His mighty deeds; Praise Him according to His excellent greatness. Praise Him with trumpet sound; Praise Him with harp and lyre. Praise Him with timbrel and dancing; Praise Him with stringed instruments and pipe. Praise Him with loud cymbals; Praise Him with resounding cymbals. Let everything that has breath praise the Lord. Praise the Lord!" (Psalm 150)

There is no way you can read the Psalms without being gripped by the celebratory aspect of worship. God is a God who deserves our praise - with our whole heart, mind, soul, and emotions. It has always struck me as funny how many people change when they come into church services. In church they are all solemn and serious.

But if you see these same people at a family dinner, an office party, birthday party or football match, they suddenly become excited and enthusiastic, and in the case of the footy match, some of them become raving lunatics. We are emotional people and emotions are very good. In church, we should always be free to be enthusiastic in our praise to God. We certainly should be joyful and happy. There is so much to be excited about.

Our text also says that the early disciples were not only enjoying joyously celebratory worship, but that they were enjoying the favour of all the people. People were impressed with this early band of joyful, loving, giving, united disciples.

The world still needs to see that we are excited about Jesus. So often the image that is portrayed is of a group of people having no fun and seeking to keep anyone else from having any fun either. But that is not Christianity – that is religion – and God hates religion!

What the church needs is a fresh revelation of the greatness of God and of the sheer number of things that our God has done for His people. Too often we walk around totally unaware of even a fraction of the blessings He has poured out upon us. If we could somehow catch a glimpse of just a small portion of the multitude of ways we have already been blessed by God, it would blow us away. We are the most blessed of all people.

Think about it. Pray about it. Ask God to show you how He has blessed you. Ask Him to reveal to you the things for which you should be thankful every day. Ask Him to give you a glimpse of His glory and a glimpse of His love for you. Such a revelation will change the way you worship. Such a revelation will change the way you live! Such a revelation will wake the sleeping giant!

I love how those in heaven praising the Lord are portrayed in the book of Revelation. Throughout the book of Revelation, we catch glimpses of this heavenly worship. The people are in the actual presence of the living God – face-to-face. John's vision transports us into heaven where we see that the chief activity is praise.

"Then I looked and heard the voice of many angels, numbering thousands upon thousands, and ten thousand times ten thousand. They encircled the throne and the living creatures and the elders. In a loud voice they sang: 'Worthy is the Lamb, who was slain, to receive power and wealth and wisdom and strength and honour and glory and praise!'" (Revelation 5:11-12)

Just think of how we will all be able to praise God when we leave this earthly kingdom and embrace the fullness of the Kingdom of heaven! How exciting is that? But what is even more exciting is the fact that we get to start that right now!

When the sleeping giant awakens, brace yourself for a wild ride as our worship explodes with life and power and joy – as the reality and power of the Kingdom of heaven explodes among us and within us.

Bring it on, Lord!

CHAPTER FIFTEEN
A Growing church

"… And the Lord added to their number daily those who were being saved." (Acts 2:47b)

I recently spent an hour or so visiting various church Web sites on the world wide web. It is fascinating to see the various slogans and mission statements that are adopted by various churches – particularly in America. Often you will find churches describing themselves as a *"friendly church."* Another well-worn saying is: *"A warm welcome awaits you."* One often used slogan I found is: *"Where everybody is somebody, and Jesus Christ is Lord!"*

Well, in one church in Jacksonville, Florida, I found a variation of that last saying which I may never forget. No doubt it was well intentioned, and I am sure the people in that church loved the Lord, but they had a slogan at the top of the page promoting their church which said, *"Where Jesus Christ is everything and everyone else is nobody!"* I couldn't believe my eyes. I also couldn't help but wonder what kind of person that slogan would attract.

There is little doubt that they had not really communicated what they wanted to say. Surely, they thought that people were in fact somebody. What they really wanted to say, probably, was that Jesus was so wonderful that in comparison to Him, everything and everyone else is secondary. It just didn't end up that way!

That slogan does point to the fact that so many churches do not think through what they are doing to reach people. In fact, many churches do not even think deeply about what they are doing. Some don't know what they are doing. And some don't even know that they should know what they're doing!

If you were to ask the average church member in Australia the question, *"Where is your church going?"* they would say something like, *"Going? Why we are not going anywhere. We've been at this location for 100 years!"*

The early church we've been focusing on in the book of Acts was a great church because it had focus. They knew that they should be doing something and they knew what that something was. These disciples had experienced the life-changing power of Jesus and had also caught a vision of how that same power could change the lives of people everywhere - and they were doing something about it.

It has been said that there are three kinds of people: those who watch what happens; those who make it happen; and those who wonder what happened! These early Christians were those who made it happen.

We have now seen that they were a regenerate church, a devoted church, an awe-filled church, a united church, a generous church, and a joyously worshipping church. Now we will see that they were an evangelistic, growing church. Notice that our text says, *"And the Lord added to their number daily those who were being saved."* These believers saw their friends, neighbours, relatives, and co-workers come to know Christ. They were at work and God was at work.

One of the first things we notice is that God was indeed active among these disciples. This is why people were being added to the church. This is always why people ultimately embrace Christ and His gift of salvation. That cannot happen unless God is at work because only God can bring someone into His kingdom. We can't save anyone. We see the sovereignty of God at work here in this early church.

Our text says that it was the Lord adding to their number. These Christians understood that people were coming to faith because the Lord Himself was doing something through His Spirit. This is something we also need to remember and depend upon. This understanding needs to be built into our approach to reaching out to people. Unless we see clearly that Jesus saves, we will have a faulty concept of evangelism and become very frustrated in the process. Additionally, we will fail to draw upon the resources of God Himself for all our evangelistic efforts and fail to spend the time in earnest prayer for unbelievers.

Of course, the reason that God is at work to reach people is that He loves people. This is why Christ came and died - for people. This is the primary reason the church exists on planet Earth - to reach people with the love of God. We are to reflect the heartbeat of God for His people, gripped by a desire to see them come to Christ and be saved. It is a desire to see their lives transformed in a positive way by the good news of God's love for them.

The question is, *"Do we desire what God desires?"* It is a question that can be very troubling. It seems that from the behaviour of most churches and Christians that we don't really desire what God desires – not strongly anyway.

George Barna's surveys indicate that fewer than one in four Christians even believe that it is their responsibility to witness to others about Jesus. Most Christians think that it is the job of the 'professionals' to evangelise. In fact, most Christians never share their faith with someone else and few have ever been involved in actually leading someone to Christ.

Dr. D. James Kennedy, founder of Evangelism Explosion, stated that, *"One of the saddest statistics of our day is that 95% of all church members have never had the joy of seeing someone come to Christ."*

It seems we are more content to be the keepers of the aquarium, than become fishers of men. What about the Great Commission? We all know it, don't we? It is where Jesus commanded us to reach out and share the good news.

> *"All authority in heaven and on earth has been given to me.*
> *Therefore, go and make disciples of all nations, baptizing them in*
> *the name of the Father and of the Son and of the Holy Spirit, and*
> *teaching them to obey everything I have commanded you. And*
> *surely I am with you always, to the very end of the age."*
> *(Matthew 28:18-20)*

This was not a suggestion; this was our purpose as His disciples. One thing is true, we need to have God do a work in our hearts to change both our minds and our behaviour.

One little girl returned home from Sunday School and expressed disappointment with the class's reaction after the day's lesson. *"We were told to go into all the world and make disciples of all nations,"* she said, *"but then we just sat there."*

During the reign of Oliver Cromwell, the British government began to run low on silver for coins. Lord Cromwell sent his men on an investigation of the local cathedral to see if they could find any precious metal there. After investigating, they reported, *"The only silver we could find is in the statues of the saints standing in the corners."* To which the radical soldier and statesman of England replied, *"Good! We will melt down the saints and put them into circulation!"* This is what may be needed today as well. The saints need to have our hearts melted with the love of God and we need to put ourselves back in circulation like the early church. Not only must God be at work, but so must we.

God is the only one Who can save, but He has chosen us to carry that message of salvation. It takes the cooperation of believers to spread the good news. God has called us into a partnership with Jesus, Who promised to build His church.

> *"Everyone who calls on the name of the Lord will be saved."* (Romans 10:13)

Those words above from the Apostle Paul are well known, but it goes on to say in the following verses, that before people can call on the Lord for help, they must believe in Him; and before they can believe in Him, they must hear about Him; and for them to hear about the Lord, someone must tell them! Look at what Paul had to say to the believers in Corinth:

> *"Therefore, if anyone is in Christ, he is a new creation; the old has gone, the new has come! All this is from God, who reconciled us to himself through Christ and gave us the ministry of reconciliation: that God was reconciling the world to himself in Christ, not counting men's sins against them. And he has committed to us the message of reconciliation. We are therefore Christ's ambassadors, as though God were making his appeal through us. We implore you on Christ's behalf: Be reconciled to God."* (2 Corinthians 5:17-20)

God wants us to participate in this ministry of reconciliation! The Bible says that this God, Who reconciled us to Himself through Jesus Christ, also gave us the ministry of reconciliation. Those of us who have been reconciled now have the privilege and the responsibility of entering into this ministry of reconciliation. But how do we do that?

We find the key when it says that God has committed to us the message of reconciliation by giving us a message to share. We have not only been given grace but the secret of grace. We have been given a message that sets others free. We have been given a message that pardons. We have been given a living, dynamic message. It is living because we have experienced its power. It is living because we have been set free by believing it.

This message is the truth of the gospel. It is the truth that anyone who believes in Jesus can be set free. It is the truth that there is no sin too black that Jesus has not already forgiven. It is the truth that there is no problem too complex that Jesus cannot solve. It is the truth that our neighbours can all be brought into God's Kingdom. It is the truth that our relatives can be reconciled to God. And we have been given this message of reconciliation.

Now it should be obvious to any of us that a message must be delivered. Someone once observed that many Christians are like the Arctic River, frozen over at the mouth. Unless we speak this message of reconciliation, others will never hear it. The greatest tragedy of all would be to have the truth that sets people free, and never to share that truth with anyone!

How can we be effective in sharing this truth? What will it take for us to begin to boldly declare the truth that will set others free? Do we need some new program? Is that the answer? I would like to propose to you that what we need is not a new program. There are already many programs for evangelism which are good. But we don't need a better understanding of a program, rather we need a better understanding of our evangelistic position. Because we have been reconciled ourselves, and have been given this message of reconciliation, we have been made ambassadors for Jesus Christ.

We read these very words in the text - *we are therefore Christ's ambassadors.* We must understand that position. We must come to see ourselves in that capacity. We are agents of reconciliation. As Christ's ambassadors we have a platform from which to speak. As an official agent of the Kingdom, we represent the King. We have a divine assignment, and we must embrace that assignment every day.

What does it really mean to function as an ambassador? It means several important things. First of all it means that we represent the King. An ambassador represents his/her government. The word of a King, Queen or Prime Minister would be passed on to a foreign government through an ambassador. The word of reconciliation with which we are entrusted is the word of our King, Jesus Christ. So, to be an ambassador also means that we are entrusted to handle the word of the King. We are entrusted to be faithful to share what the King desires us to share. We must be accurate with His words. We must be faithful to share them and to make sure they are clearly understood.

As an ambassador we are also privileged to carry the authority of the King. When our ambassador speaks for our government, that speech carries the authority of our government. When we speak for King Jesus, our speech carries the authority of Jesus. When we offer salvation on the terms revealed in God's Word, we can be sure that when people respond to our word on behalf of our King, our King will back up His word.

This is why that text says that when we speak, it is as though God were making His appeal through us. We are speaking on Christ's behalf. We stand in the place of Christ when we embrace this ministry of reconciliation. We are agents of the Kingdom. We are Christ's ambassadors.

Until we see ourselves as agents of the Kingdom, ambassadors for Christ, we will miss most of the opportunities that present themselves every day. What we read in this text is a radically new way of thinking about ourselves. We have heard the words before, and because of that they may not have the impact they should. We need to hear them with fresh insight today.

We need to ask God to create in us this mentality of being an ambassador. As agents of the Kingdom, we are to infiltrate every walk of life. As ambassadors for Christ, we are to represent our King and faithfully share His word to all people. We have been reconciled so we can participate in seeing others reconciled. We have been shown the way so that we can show others the way.

Many years ago now, an artist, seeking to depict on canvas the meaning of evangelism, painted this storm at sea. Black clouds filled the sky. Illuminated by a flash of lightning, a little boat could be seen disintegrating under the pounding of the ocean. Men were struggling in the swirling waters, their anguished faces crying out for help. The only glimmer of hope appeared in the foreground of the painting, where a large rock protruded out of the water. There, clutching desperately with both hands, was one lone seaman. It was a moving scene.

Looking at the painting, one could see in the tempest a symbol of mankind's hopeless condition. And, true to the Gospel, the only hope of salvation was 'the Rock of Ages,' a shelter in the time of storm. However, as the artist reflected more on his work, he realised that the painting did not accurately portray his subject. So, he discarded the canvas, and painted another one. It was very similar to the first: the black clouds, the flashing lightning, the angry waters, the little boat crushed by the pounding waves, and the crew vainly struggling in the water. In the foreground the seaman was clutching the large rock for salvation. But the artist made one small change: the survivor was holding on with only one hand, and with the other hand he was reaching down to pull up a drowning friend. Now the artist was happy.

In Jesus' name please hear this. We are safe! We are on the rock! We made it. Praise be to God! But what about all the others floating by? What about our comrades in the broken, beaten boat of life that is simply not going to last the distance and get them to safety? From our position of safety, are we prepared to get wet and help them out of the water, or are we just content to enjoy the safety of the rock without rescuing as many of our brother and sisters as we can?

I have deliberately not talked about evangelistic methods. Nor have I exhorted you to race out there tomorrow and share the four spiritual laws with a neighbour! My purpose here is simply to shake us up enough for the Holy Spirit to awaken something within our hearts. There must be a change in our hearts before we even contemplate how we are going to be salt and light in our community and our nation.

It is my very firm belief that the methods and the vehicles for evangelism will come. As I have shared many times before in my ministry, the most powerful tool we have is our own testimony – our own story of what God has done in our lives. That is the most effective way of reaching those around us.

If we know that the Lord Who came to seek and to save the lost has entrusted us with the same holy mission and that this is the primary reason for us still being on this planet; if that truth starts to take root and gets a hook into our heart; then, and only then, will we begin to see captives set free and the kingdom of God grow beyond our wildest expectations. Then and only then will the once sleeping giant, turn the world upside down again!

God will add to our number daily, those who are being saved, when we embrace our calling as ministers of reconciliation in Christ, through Christ and for Christ.

CHAPTER SIXTEEN
A Healing Touch

I love the story of the arrogant, prideful lion, who wanted to remind other animals how great he was. He went to the gazelle and roared, "*Who is the king of the jungle?*" Trembling, the gazelle answered, "*Why, you are, mighty lion.*" He went next to the giraffe and roared, "*Who is the king of the jungle?*" Fearful, the giraffe answered, "*Why, you are, mighty lion.*" Next, he went to the monkey and roared, "*Who is the king of the jungle?*" Startled, the monkey answered, "*Why, you are mighty lion.*" Finally, he went to the elephant and roared, "*Who is the king of the jungle?*" The elephant reached out, grabbed the lion with his trunk, slammed the lion to the ground several times, and flung him hard into a large boulder. As the lion lay there in shock and pain, he finally said to the elephant, "*Just because you didn't know the answer, you didn't have to take it so personally!*"

Power is one of the most sought-after prizes in life. But when people get it, often the results are not that positive. Power tends to corrupt both the people who have it and the people who feel its effect. Too often people use power to abuse, belittle, subdue, conquer, and even destroy others. In the process, they find that they become those people whom no one likes; miserable people, corrupted from the inside out. Power has a decidedly negative side. But it can have a positive impact as well.

On that incredible Day of Pentecost that we read about in Acts 2, power from heaven came upon the people. The power of God turned despairing doubters into dynamic disciples. They had received the promised Holy Spirit and were clothed with power from on high. But power for what? Did they receive the power of God simply so they could feel good about themselves? Did they receive the power of God to keep it to themselves? No! They received the power of God to energise them to be witnesses to Jesus Christ in a secular society. The power of Pentecost was for people; to enable the disciples to reach out and touch human need and share the liberating truth of the Gospel of Christ.

The power of Pentecost is to cure the paralysis of the world. It's all about caring for people. The power of the Spirit is not given so we can turn inward and become exclusive as we enjoy the company of other Spirit-filled people. Unfortunately, many who have experienced a personal Pentecost in their own lives have established these little exclusive societies, complete with their own sub-culture and jargon.

The questions, *"Are you charismatic?"* or *"Have you been filled with the Spirit?"* are often the critical questions. But those are really not the important questions. The questions should be:

"Has the Spirit's filling given you a ministry?"
"How has the power of God enabled you to reach out to others?"
"How have the gifts of the Spirit enabled you to communicate the Gospel of Christ to human hearts?"

Pentecost is for the sake of the world. We must never be content to sing "Standing on the Promises" while all we're doing is sitting in the premises. Pentecost happened to enable us to reach out and touch others.

But how do you share the Gospel with people in this upwardly mobile, secular society, especially those who appear to be so self-sufficient? Doesn't it seem easier to share the Gospel with people who seem to be in desperate need; someone who has hit bottom; a wretched sinner who has nowhere to turn, who's flat on his back? It seems easier to share with that kind of person than those who live in our neighbourhood, who are affluent and appear to have everything they need. The kind of people I'm speaking of all have nice houses, manicured lawns, at least two nice cars, fine clothes, children who are doing well in school, great jobs, and plenty of money. What more could they need?

The truth is, things are not always what they seem. The down-and-out and the up-and-out have at least two things in common: They are both human and they both have deep needs. Inside every one of those nice houses sitting on their manicured lawns are people who hurt, people who have unmet personal needs and people who need a touch from God.

In our next text, we see the power of God healing a human life. We see people who have been touched by the power of God, now touching others. It is the story of the lame man who begged by the gate called Beautiful. In this passage we see a real example of the power of God to heal. This man was healed physically, but the message of this text is not limited to physical healing in any way. This passage deals with human transformation. Here, we will find valuable lessons which I pray will motivate us to find opportunities to minister to hurting people.

> *"One day Peter and John were going up to the temple at the time of prayer – at three in the afternoon. Now a man who was lame from birth was being carried to the temple gate called Beautiful, where he was put every day to beg from those going into the temple courts. When he saw Peter and John about to enter, he asked them for money. Peter looked straight at him, as did John. Then Peter said, "Look at us!" So, the man gave them his attention, expecting to get something from them. Then Peter said, "Silver or gold I do not have, but what I do have I give you. In the name of Jesus Christ of Nazareth, walk." Taking him by the right hand, he helped him up, and instantly the man's feet and ankles became strong. He jumped to his feet and began to walk. Then he went with them into the temple courts, walking and jumping, and praising God."(Acts 3:1-8)*

What we see before us is a human tragedy. Notice firstly the misfortune of this man. The Scripture tells us that this man was crippled. But more than that, this man was crippled *from birth*. Think about the tragedy of that for a moment. He had never been able to stand and walk, to run and play like the other boys. His parents had to carry him absolutely everywhere. So many opportunities were denied him because of his affliction. Now, he's a grown man and every day friends must carry him to the Temple so he can beg for a living. A tragic situation indeed. We can only speculate concerning what effect this must have had on his heart. He could easily have been bitter. There had never been a day in his life when he had not been a burden to somebody. He could not walk; he could not work. All he could do was sit there, beg and hope that people would have pity on him.

This man symbolises for us the reality of tragedy in life. As we look at him, we are reminded of the fact that everywhere we look there is human hurt, human suffering, and human tragedy. Sometimes it manifests itself through a physical affliction such as this man had, but more often it goes unseen to human eyes.

For each one who is crippled physically, we find thousands more who are crippled emotionally, and hundreds of thousands who are crippled spiritually. The message of this man is that there are needs to be met in human lives everywhere. And those needs also exist in lives that are outwardly wonderful.

This lame man sat and begged at the gate called "*Beautiful.*" From all historical accounts, we know that this gate was indeed an impressive sight. Much of it was made from Corinthian bronze. It was inlaid with ornately decorated gold. As the sun would shine upon it, its glistening brightness could be seen for miles. Yet, sitting under a magnificent, beautiful creation we find this pathetic, sad, suffering human being.

How many of our co-workers, friends or neighbours appear outwardly to be doing OK, yet inwardly they are struggling? They are over-extended financially. They don't know what to do with their children. Their marriages are falling apart. Their job is hanging by a thread. They've lost all self-esteem. They're guilty and depressed and don't know where to turn. Behind every door there is human need. Every person has a story to tell. We've all been hurt; we've all been used; we've all failed; and we all need healing. We need Jesus - and that's the biggest need that anyone has. People need a heavenly touch from God.

What this man by the gate needed, indeed, what all people need, is a heavenly touch from God. He needed the power of Pentecost to be made available to him. But how was he going to get that? Every day he came to the Temple. Every day he sat and begged. He wasn't in the group at Pentecost. He didn't know what was going on. He lived his life away from the mainstream. He was oblivious to the good news of God. He couldn't get to church, and I'm not sure he would have gone if he could. Why should he go? What was there for him?

Unfortunately, this is the attitude of many people today. They hurt, but they hurt in silence, not being willing to share their intimate hurts with anyone else. The church is the last place they want to go. Many of them view the church as this judgmental community of self-righteous hypocrites. But even if they have a good view of the church, there's not much to motivate them to drag their tired bones out of bed on a Sunday morning in order to come alone to one of its services. This crippled man may have been like that. Who would bring him a heavenly touch?

Jesus had ascended into heaven but He sent the Holy Spirit to empower his people so they could be His messengers. And here we find two such messengers: Peter and John. What an unlikely pair, Peter and John. Normally it was Peter and Andrew, and James and John. That is how we usually find them in the Gospels. Peter and John were so different naturally, but Christ had brought these two together. Their friendship had turned into fellowship and they were now Christ's ambassadors.

So, we find these ambassadors coming to the Temple to pray at the ninth hour, which was three in the afternoon. On their way, they encounter this crippled man who is begging for money. He has been there every day. No doubt they have seen him before. In fact, he was probably there when Jesus passed by. But Jesus had not healed him. Strange? Perhaps. We don't know why. Undoubtedly, God had His reasons. It could have been that God wanted to use this man as an illustration of His grace at this time.

As Peter and John were going in, he began to ask them for money and they stopped. Look at the motivation of these messengers. They saw in this man an opportunity to minister the touch of God. Their lives had been turned around by Jesus and now they wanted to share what they had received with others. That was their motivation. And because of that, they weren't in a hurry. They had time for people. After all, Jesus always did. In the midst of His busy schedule, He always had time for the individual. His motivation for ministry was people and so was theirs now. What was the ministry of these messengers? Their ministry was to bring a heavenly touch to a human tragedy.

So, they stopped and said to the man, "*Look at us.*" He looked at them thinking they would give him some money. And what they said next is interesting. Then Peter said, "*Silver or gold I do not have, but what I have I give you. In the name of Jesus Christ of Nazareth, walk.*"

What tis man wanted was money, but what this man needed was healing. And so, Peter told him they didn't have what he wanted but they certainly had what he really needed. He wanted to fill his cup, but God wanted to fill his heart. He wanted a handout, but he was about to receive a hand up.

"*Taking him by the right hand, he helped him up, and instantly the man's feet and ankles became strong.*" Notice that Peter didn't just share about Christ. He reached out to do something for this man. The heavenly touch comes through human messengers, who are motivated by the love of God. If we are going to touch people with God's presence, we must be there where they are, reaching out to them, helping them in the way they need help.

But notice that they could only give this man what they had. Peter said, "*But what I have I give to you.*" Peter could not give him silver and gold because he had none. He could only give what he had. So it is with us. If we do not possess a living relationship with Jesus Christ, we will never be able to impart that heavenly touch to others. You can only impart what you actually possess. It is important that we take care to develop our own spiritual life if we would impart spiritual life to others.

We must be careful not to let the things of this world get in the way. There is an old story of Thomas Aquinas when he visited Pope Innocent II and found him counting a large sum of money.

"*Ah, Thomas,*" said the Pope, "*the church can no longer say, 'silver and gold have I none.'*"

"*That is true, Your Holiness,*" said Aquinas, "*but then, neither can it now say, 'Arise and walk.'*"

These two disciples didn't have silver and gold, but they had the power of God. What we need is not possessions, but power: Power to touch people's lives with the presence of the living God; power to reach out to people and lift them up out of their tragic circumstances and give them hope and healing, friendship and fellowship. This was the ministry of these messengers and this is our ministry as well.

When a heavenly touch encounters a human tragedy, the result is a healing transformation! That is what occurred in the case of this lame man. A miracle happened to him. Let's look at the manifestation of that miracle.

Verse 8 says, "*He jumped to his feet and began to walk.*" When Peter took him by the hand, something happened. Peter was not content with merely sharing with him. He reached out in a physical way to encourage this man to take a huge leap of faith. Sometimes we have to do that for others too. We have to resort to action to encourage them to take a step toward Jesus. When Peter did this, the man was healed. His need was met. His legs were strengthened. He stood to his feet. He was made whole. He took a step of faith because Peter and John had taken a step of faith. And Jesus met them all there and did what was needed.

There was a metamorphosis as a result of this miracle. The man was completely transformed. Not only was he healed, but joy flooded his soul. The Scripture says, "*Then he went with them into the temple courts, walking and jumping, and praising God.*" Because someone cared enough to reach out to him in the name of Jesus, his life had been totally transformed.

What did this mean to him? It meant now that he could walk. It meant that he could work. It meant that he could live a full life. But it meant more than that – much, much more. It meant that somebody cared. It meant that God loved him. Now he could live in communion with God every day. He had been healed in more ways than one. How could he help but rejoice? And that is precisely what he did. He was walking and leaping and praising God. I'd say he was excited. And so should we be!

It's OK to be excited. There are thousands of lifeless saints sitting in churches across the nation who think they are dignified when, really, they are petrified. They have lost their leap and they need to get it back and get excited like this guy was. That's what can happen to you when you encounter a touch from God. He can reach into our hearts and heal all our human tragedy. He can liberate us and empower us to liberate others.

The real message to us here is that we have been empowered for the sake of other people. There are needs all around us. There are many needs in our church fellowship. And there is nothing more important among God's priorities than people. All that we do is to share the healing power of God with human beings so they may be liberated to serve the living God.

Look around you each day in your circle of influence. See the needs. Ask yourself, "*What are the needs of this person and what can I do to minister to those needs?*" Of course, the goal is to lead people to Jesus. But we must first reach out to them in a way which touches their need. We must give them what we have - our time, our friendship, ourselves. As we do, their ears will be opened and their hearts receptive to hearing about the Good News - and when they receive that, like the man who was healed, they will be walking and leaping and praising God!

Are you with me here? Do you really believe that the same power which created this entire universe; the power which raised Jesus from the dead; the power which keeps the sun burning with life-giving energy 24 hours a day – is the power which is in you? If Christ is in you, then the greatest power in the universe is within you! There is not a single need known to mankind that cannot be met by the power of the living God – and you have that power!

There are literally thousands of people surrounding us every day who need what we have. Will we take the time to share it with them? May God give us people to touch with the power of God.

CHAPTER SEVENTEEN
Overcoming Intimidation

I want us to begin this chapter by digesting a rather large section of the text in Acts. I could write a whole book on just these 31 verses, but I will just extract some of the key truths here for us which impact how we live and what we value.

> *"The priests and the captain of the temple guard and the Sadducees came up to Peter and John while they were speaking to the people. They were greatly disturbed because the apostles were teaching the people, proclaiming in Jesus the resurrection of the dead. They seized Peter and John and, because it was evening, they put them in jail until the next day. But many who heard the message believed; so the number of men who believed grew to about five thousand.*
>
> *The next day the rulers, the elders and the teachers of the law met in Jerusalem. Annas the high priest was there, and so were Caiaphas, John, Alexander and others of the high priest's family. They had Peter and John brought before them and began to question them: 'By what power or what name did you do this?' Then Peter, filled with the Holy Spirit, said to them: "Rulers and elders of the people! If we are being called to account today for an act of kindness shown to a man who was lame and are being asked how he was healed, then know this, you and all the people of Israel: It is by the name of Jesus Christ of Nazareth, whom you crucified but whom God raised from the dead, that this man stands before you healed.*
>
> *Jesus is 'the stone you builders rejected, which has become the cornerstone.' Salvation is found in no one else, for there is no other name under heaven given to mankind by which we must be saved. When they saw the courage of Peter and John and realized that they were unschooled, ordinary men, they were astonished and they took note that these men had been with Jesus. But since they could see the man who had been healed standing there with them, there was nothing they could say.*

So they ordered them to withdraw from the Sanhedrin and then conferred together. 'What are we going to do with these men?' they asked. 'Everyone living in Jerusalem knows they have performed a notable sign, and we cannot deny it. But to stop this thing from spreading any further among the people, we must warn them to speak no longer to anyone in this name.'

Then they called them in again and commanded them not to speak or teach at all in the name of Jesus. But Peter and John replied, 'Which is right in God's eyes: to listen to you, or to him? You be the judges! As for us, we cannot help speaking about what we have seen and heard.'

After further threats they let them go. They could not decide how to punish them, because all the people were praising God for what had happened. For the man who was miraculously healed was over forty years old. On their release, Peter and John went back to their own people and reported all that the chief priests and the elders had said to them.

When they heard this, they raised their voices together in prayer to God. "Sovereign Lord," they said, "you made the heavens and the earth and the sea, and everything in them. You spoke by the Holy Spirit through the mouth of your servant, our father David:

'Why do the nations rage and the peoples plot in vain? The kings of the earth rise up and the rulers band together against the Lord and against his anointed one. Indeed, Herod and Pontius Pilate met together with the Gentiles and the people of Israel in this city to conspire against your holy servant Jesus, whom you anointed. They did what your power and will had decided beforehand should happen.

Now, Lord, consider their threats and enable your servants to speak your word with great boldness. Stretch out your hand to heal and perform signs and wonders through the name of your holy servant Jesus.' After they prayed, the place where they were meeting was shaken. And they were all filled with the Holy Spirit and spoke the word of God boldly." (Acts 4:1-31)

Lots of us like to be temporarily frightened. There is a certain thrill at being shocked by a scene in a scary movie. A little scare may be fun, but real fear can take over the human psyche. It is such a powerful force that it can control a human being. Taken to the extreme, it can even kill. The expression, 'scared to death' can become a reality in certain circumstances for some people. Some are totally immobilised by fear. To them, fear becomes a bondage, a prison from which they find no escape.

Of course, our society likes to categorise the fears we have. We want to make every human malady and problem a sickness of some kind, so we define it in 'scientific' terms. In this case a fear becomes a phobia. The word phobia is in vogue today to describe all sorts of fears which afflict different people. There are literally hundreds, if not thousands of phobias. One phobia was made familiar to us all by Steven Spielberg in his movie by the same name - *Arachnophobia*, the fear of spiders.

Can you guess what some of the other phobias are? I have a brief list here just to bore you or edify you.

Claustrophobia: the fear of enclosed places
Acrophobia: the fear of high places
Agoraphobia: the fear of open places
Anthropophobia: the fear of people.

There are all kinds of obscure phobias:

Bacteriophobia, the fear of bacteria
Zoophobia: the fear of animals
Eisopetrophobia: the fear of mirrors
Aurophobia: the fear of gold
Metophobia: the fear of money
Telephonophoboa: the fear of the telephone
Blennophobia: the fear of slime
Musophobia: the fear of mice
Microphobia: fear of small things
Neophobia: the fear of new things
Monophobia: the fear of one thing
Pantophobia: the fear of everything

There are still more …

Scotophobia: the fear of darkness
Carcinophobia: the fear of cancer
Hydrophobophobia: the fear of rabies
Algophobia: the fear of pain
Kinetophobia: the fear of motion
Tachophobia: the fear of speed
Autophobia: the fear of being alone
Hypegiaphobia: the fear of responsibility
Kakorraphiaphobia: the fear of failure
Gametophobia: the fear of marriage … and even
Phobophobia: the fear of fear
Triskaidekaphobia: the fear of the number thirteen
Oikophobia: the fear of home
Thanathophobia: the fear of death
Ouranophobia: the fear of heaven
Stygiophobia: the fear of hell
Peccatiphobia: the fear of sin … and of course …
Ecclesiophobia: the fear of church.

There are hundreds of fears and the list grows each day. The mere existence of such a list reminds us that we live in a fearful society, and many people are in bondage to it. We all have a tendency to fear. It is a weakness in the human race and it can be a real problem for us as we seek to serve Jesus Christ.

The enemy of God and the Christian faith is Satan, and he uses fear against us and to keep us from fully following Jesus. This process is known as intimidation. To intimidate is defined as 'to make timid or fearful.' Intimidation is a strategy of Satan by which he seeks to control people.

People in the world who do not know Christ often seek to control Christians through intimidation. As we attempt to live biblical Christianity in a secular society, we will come face to face with intimidation. The real question is what will we do when we face intimidation? Will we yield to fear, or will we find a way to overcome intimidation?

The Apostles wrestled with the same question because they faced intimidation every day in their ministry. As they sought to share the Gospel of Christ and win the world to Jesus, they had to come to grips with the intimidation of the world. In our text above, we see such a situation and we also find valuable lessons in how to conquer the intimidation which we face.

In Acts chapter 1, the promise is given by Jesus that the disciples would receive power. In Acts 2, on the day of Pentecost, they receive that power. It was the power to become mighty witnesses for Jesus Christ. Thousands of people were saved that day and the power of God was unleashed. In Acts 3, we see the power of God used to help people. The man by the Temple gate called Beautiful was healed.

Now, in Acts 4, we see the fallout of that healing among the religious leaders of the day. What we see here is a confused interrogation. The religious leaders didn't know what to do. They had never encountered this kind of situation. The power of God had come down, and now they had to deal with these people who were the obvious channels of that power.

The believers had been filled with the power of the Holy Spirit and were now proceeding to live as Jesus' disciples in their secular society. Whenever that kind of radical transformation takes place, it always causes a stir.

People living in the power of God stand out in the crowd, and the world doesn't quite know what to do with them. Hence the confused query of the religious leaders in verse 16, *"What are we going to do with these men?"* They didn't know how to respond. God's power had manifested, and God's people were now on the move. Things were happening! Things these religious leaders had not counted on. The disciples were preaching boldly in the name of Jesus.

A notable healing had taken place right under their noses and they couldn't deny it. What would they do with these men now? They didn't have the answer. They were in a state of confusion.

The question they asked is the same question the world asks today. Just as the religious leaders did not know how to respond, so the world does not know how to respond.

When a Christian attempts to live as God intended, he or she stands out. When a believer attempts to live with high moral standards in honesty and integrity, in purity and holiness, refusing to engage in any activity or conversation which would violate the principles of God's Word or hamper their testimony, this kind of person will always across the grain of broken, secular society like ours.

What does the world do in response? I believe the tactics of the world are predictable. The first thing they do is try and ignore us. They simply act like we are not here. If they can't ignore us, their next strategy is to belittle us, or at least belittle our faith. If belittling doesn't work, they seek to intimidate and threaten us. They try to use their power or position to control and manipulate us into giving our Christianity a lower profile. This is how they attempt to answer the question, *"What shall we do with these Christians?"*

In Acts 4 we find the religious leaders deliberating on a plan of intimidation. They concluded that the proper course of action would be to warn Peter and John to quit preaching about Jesus - and that's what they proceeded to do. Little did they know what kind of men they were now dealing with. These were no longer the timid men who had fled in fear when Jesus was arrested. They were a whole new breed altogether now.

The religious leaders were about to encounter men who now had courage. Peter and John would no longer be intimidated. They knew in Whom they believed and were persuaded that He was able to keep them in the centre of His will. Lives that had been marked by cowardice and fear were now marked by confidence and boldness. The religious leaders noticed this confidence. In verse 13 it says, *"When they saw the courage of Peter and John and realised that they were unschooled, ordinary men, they were astonished and they took note that these men had been with Jesus."*

But while they recognised the confidence of Peter and John, they still thought they could intimidate them. So, they called them in again and commanded them not to speak or teach at all in the name of Jesus. But Peter and John replied, *"Judge for yourselves whether it is right in God's sight to obey you rather than God. For we cannot help speaking about what we have seen and heard."* After further threats they let them go.

Their tactic was simple, and it is still the tactic the world uses today: If you can't ignore the Christians, intimidate them. The goal, of course, is to get these Christians to cool it when it comes to living out their faith in the world around them.

Notice that the religious leaders were willing to let these men believe anything they chose. What they were not willing to let them do was to act on what they believed. That is precisely what the world tells us today. *"We respect your right to your religious belief, just don't impose that belief on anyone else."*

The fact of the matter is that we can't really impose anything on anyone. But that's not what they mean. What they mean is that they do not want us acting on what we believe. They don't want us talking about what we believe. They certainly don't want us trying to influence other people to believe what we believe. And when we live out what we believe and stand up for what we believe, they feel threatened, so they seek to threaten us. They just want us to calm down, get us to lay low and to blend in.

Peter and John would have nothing to do with such attempts to stifle or control the Spirit within them. They said that they could not stop speaking what they had seen and heard. In essence, they told the religious leaders that they had to obey God rather than men. They didn't say they would not stop speaking, they said they could not stop - it wasn't their choice. They saw it as obedience to God's command. It was not God's suggestion that they be witnesses, they saw it as God's command. They had no choice but to obey. *"For we cannot help speaking about what we have seen and heard."* We see here evidence of the confidence and courage which now filled these disciples.

But we must not miss the truth that this was a tense situation. They were speaking to the highest religious authorities of the day. It was a very fearful thing to be dragged before the great Sanhedrin court. These were the same leaders who had been implicated in the death of Jesus. Who was to say the same wouldn't happen to His disciples? This was a fearful situation which they faced. But face it they did - in the power of God.

We face situations like this in our lives as we seek to live out our Christian faith in a secular society. We have to face our family, our friends, our neighbours, our co-workers, our employers. We face the people with whom we do business; our clients, our customers; the mechanic who works on our car; the shopkeepers who sell us our clothes and our food and the list goes on. We must relate to people in the society in which we live, and at times we are intimidated by them because we are afraid of how they may respond to our faith.

The problem is, when we are intimidated, we feel like we have somehow failed the Lord. We don't feel good about ourselves, and we vow to do better next time. But the good news is we don't have to feel that way. We can face our fears and overcome them. We can live in the boldness of the power of God. We can make a difference in the lives of others. We can turn our community upside down for Jesus Christ. We can have the same confidence and boldness that Peter and John had in the face of fears which could have immobilised them. We have the same resource which was available to them, and I believe we have the same desire to be bold witnesses which was theirs. If we desire boldness as they did, we must go to the same source they did.

The confidence of Peter and John was the result of them having been with Jesus. So, when they needed more boldness and more confidence, they came to Jesus again to receive it.

> *"Now, Lord, consider their threats and enable your servants to speak your word with great boldness. Stretch out your hand to heal and perform miraculous signs and wonders through the name of your holy servant Jesus."*

How do you face intimidation and overcome it? You do so by drawing on the same resource by which you live the Christian life. Jesus is that resource. He is the power by which we live. He is the power by which we witness. He is the power by which we become confident and bold. He is the power by which we face intimidation victoriously. When the first disciples of Jesus Christ needed power, they understood they needed prayer - and so they prayed.

In their prayer, we see several important elements. Firstly, they did not assume that they should have to bear these threats alone. They asked God to take note of the threats. This threatening situation was God's problem, not theirs, and so they laid that problem at God's feet. The implication is that God would do something about it.

Secondly, they prayed that they would be given confidence to speak God's word. The quest of the early church was to be able to confidently spread the Good News about Jesus Christ. That should still be the quest of the church today. Thirdly, they prayed that God would act in a way that only God could, to touch the lives of people.

Now you had better be careful when you pray this kind of prayer. This is the kind of prayer that God loves to answer! He certainly answered them that day. The Scripture says that after they prayed, the place where they were meeting was shaken. And they were all filled with the Holy Spirit and spoke the word of God boldly.

Here the evidence of being filled with the Holy Spirit is that they were now emboldened to speak the Word of God. They faced intimidation, they turned to the Lord, and intimidation turned into boldness. It happened then, and it can happen today.

Intimidation comes from many sources, but one of the greatest sources of intimidation for the Christian is the fear of facing people s we share the Gospel message of Christ. It's a fear the Devil seeks to feed, but it's a fear we do not have to endure.

God has called us to into boldness. We can face intimidation in the power of Jesus Christ and overcome it. We, too, can become confident and bold, as we share the life-changing Gospel of Christ. But we must go to the only resource which counts. We must go to Jesus and draw upon our relationship with Him for strength. Then we must act. We must speak in His name and watch Him work.

You can't receive courage, confidence, and boldness by listening to a six-part series on the subject. The answer is not found in a seminar. In the final analysis, this kind of boldness comes as a by-product of our relationship with Jesus. It sounds so simple, almost too simple. But the paradox of the Christian life is that it *is* simple. The Christian life is both impossible and easy at the same time. It is complex and simple. It is impossible to live the Christian life in our own power, but it's easy to live in His power. It is complex and beyond our comprehension but simple in that all you must do is surrender to Jesus and let Him figure it all out.

Whatever intimidation you might face, you can face it with faith and boldness in Jesus Christ. You can rise above intimidation and overcome it through the power that comes from knowing the Lord. Flee to Jesus. You will always find refuge and strength in Him.

CHAPTER EIGHTEEN
One Heart and Mind

It has been said that when humanity fell from grace, we inherited not only a tendency to hide from God, but a tendency to hide from each other as well. We struggle with conflicting desires. On the one hand, we desire to be close to one another, and on the other hand, we want to hold each other at arm's length. We have learned to be suspicious of other people's motives. At times we've been burned and so we fear being burned again and so we build barriers which effectively insulate us from one another and they become an obstacle to true unity in the church.

We read in John 17 where Jesus prayed that we might be one, even as He and the Father are one. But for that to happen, many barriers have to fall. Suspicion has to be replaced with openness; uncertainty has to be replaced with willingness; and fear has to be replaced with love. On that famous day of Pentecost when the church was born, that is precisely what happened - the barriers came crashing down. The Holy Spirit of God moved in and produced a wonderful unity in that first group of believers.

> *"All the believers were one in heart and mind. No one claimed that any of their possessions was their own, but they shared everything they had. With great power the apostles continued to testify to the resurrection of the Lord Jesus. And God's grace was so powerfully at work in them all that there were no needy persons among them. For from time to time those who owned land or houses sold them, brought the money from the sales and put it at the apostles' feet, and it was distributed to anyone who had need. Joseph, a Levite from Cyprus, whom the apostles called Barnabas (which means 'son of encouragement'), sold a field he owned and brought the money and put it at the apostles' feet."* (Acts 4:32-37)

Our text above describes the extent of that unity as it existed at the very beginning. For a while, they were allowed to live in the glorious oneness which only the Spirit can produce.

I believe this oneness can be found where people truly allow Christ to be Lord and surrender to the leading of the Holy Spirit in their personal lives. I also believe that deep down within us, we all long to be close, to be part of the same family, to be in tune and in touch with one another. As we look at this passage of Scripture above, let's see what kind of unity the Spirit produced in this young church and what kind of unity He can produce in us today.

"All the believers were one in heart and mind." (Acts 4:32a)

When the Spirit of God took charge of the lives of these disciples on the day of Pentecost, He produced a mystical unity among them. The believers were experiencing a new unity which they did not produce. The diverse multitude which had gathered from all nations and tongues had been melted together by divine love into a union that was both mystical in nature and divine in origin. Those things which divided them before had faded into insignificance. They had met the Lord Jesus through His Spirit. They were together and they were one.

Notice the three words mentioned in the first part of this verse: the words *believers*, *heart* and *mind*. Their new-found unity could be seen in three areas which these words reveal to us. It was a unity of faith, a unity of emotions, and a unity of will.

Notice that these 'believers' were one. They were one with each other because they believed the same thing. They had placed their faith in Jesus and were now attempting to live out that faith together. There can be no fellowship without a shared belief.

"But if we walk in the light as he is in the light, we have fellowship with one another." (1 John 1:7)

It is only as we walk in the light of the truth of God's Word that we can enjoy true fellowship with one another. A common faith unites us. The prophet Amos asked that very simple question many years beforehand:

"Do two walk together unless they have agreed to do so?" (Amos 3:3)

They were not only united by their faith, but they were also united in heart. Their faith had brought them together and now their every desire was to follow Jesus Christ. They desired to express His love and to share that love with every human being they met. What had begun in faith had made its way to their hearts. They not only believed it intellectually and accepted it by faith, but they knew it to be true experientially.

These disciples had experienced the love of Jesus Christ and the power of the Holy Spirit. They had been given new life and their hearts were full of joy. They were excited about their faith. Because of the love of Jesus for them, they had fallen in love with Him; and along with Him, every other believer as well. Now they could call one another 'brother' and 'sister' because they were part of the same family. They could now express love, care and concern for one another freely and openly. The barriers had fallen down and they were one - one in faith and one in heart.

They were also one in mind. The mind has to do with our will. The mind has to do with our decision-making processes. What had happened on the day Pentecost was not only to affect their hearts, but also to affect their thinking. They not only believed alike, and desired alike to follow Jesus, but they made a decision to do so together. They decided to follow through on what had happened to them. They were willing to acknowledge Jesus as their Lord and Saviour, and all the other disciples as their family.

If we, as the church of Jesus Christ, are ever going to express the unity of the Spirit, we must not only desire to do so, but we must also decide to do so. There must be an act of our will in order to follow through on the desire we have to be one.

They had made this decision and they declared it publicly. It says, in the last part of verse 32, "No one claimed that any of his possessions was his own, but they shared everything they had." They acknowledged to one another that they were one. They said, "What's mine is yours; what's yours is mine. We're together in this thing." That's a powerful acknowledgement of unity and it's also a powerful demonstration of the reality of that unity.

Only God could achieve all of this. This was a mystical unity, something born of God, begun by the Holy Spirit and carried on in His power. Is it possible to possess this kind of unity today? I believe it is. But again, it's not something which is produced by human plans. It is something which can only be achieved by the power of the Spirit of God working in the hearts of people who are committed to Him.

If we had to depend on human beings to produce this unity, we would quickly despair. There is too much selfishness and self-centeredness within us to pull it off. But because this unity is a mystical unity, a unity produced by God through the power of His Spirit, then we have hope. We can possess this kind of unity if we will yield to the Holy Spirit to produce it in us. We must surrender to Him and desire His will for our life.

> *"With great power the apostles continued to testify to the resurrection of the Lord Jesus. And God's grace was so powerfully at work in them all …" (Acts 4:33)*

We now move from a mystical unity to a ministerial unity. These people were not only one in spirit, but they were also one in purpose, and their purpose was to preach the Gospel to every person they encountered. The powerful Sanhedrin had warned them not to speak any more in the name of Jesus, but were they afraid? Far from it! By the power of the Holy Spirit working in their lives, they were more united than ever to get the job done.

It says here that the Apostles were giving witness "*with great power.*" It says further, that "*God's grace was so powerfully at work in them all..*" They were experiencing great power and great grace. Because of the great power which they now possessed, they could give effective and powerful witness to the grace of God. And when they did, even greater grace was upon them.

The grace and power of God produced a living witness - and a living witness produced even more grace. There is nothing quite like a church which is united in purpose. A unity in terms of our ministry produces an even greater unity among us.

That is why it is so important to move from a mystical unity of spirit into the practical unity of purpose. Otherwise, we will quickly become inward and introspective. When that happens, it's only a matter of time before we lose the unity altogether. The whole purpose of our being one, is not to bask in our oneness, but to join together with a common purpose. There is work to be done. There is a Great Commission to be fulfilled. That is why Jesus birthed the church on earth and left us here to fulfill His mission. That is why He made us of one heart and soul.

Not only will we be able to maintain the unity of the Spirit if we are of one purpose, but we will be able, because we are united, to fulfill that purpose in a powerful way. Those Christians who are united are the Christians who are accomplishing something for Jesus Christ. I believe that all significant, effective ministry can only be done by those who are united in their desire to see that ministry done. A congregation can have a great location; committed leaders; excellent facilities; fantastic parking; lots of people attending and plenty of money; but still be ineffective in reaching their community for Christ.

On the other hand, I know some church fellowships which are quite small; hard to find; with pastors who have no real formal training; with only a handful of leaders; meeting in inadequate facilities; and are always struggling to pay the bills; but they literally exploded as they reached person after person for Jesus Christ. They did so because they decided to come together with a united purpose to do something for Jesus Christ. Their human resources were meagre, but their divine resources were infinite. Because of their unity, they were able to tap into the divine resources they needed.

In this area of unity and purpose, it is so vitally important that we understand the place of decision. Our mystical unity comes as the result of the Holy Spirit's action in our lives. Our ministerial unity comes from our decision to pull together. If our church is going to have this essential unity of purpose, then we need everyone on board, pulling together, sharing the load. We have to decide that the overall purpose for which we are striving is important enough to give ourselves to it fully.

We must decide that we are going to give more than our spare time to this endeavour; we will become supportive, involved, active participants, moving in the direction God is leading us.

We also see there was a material unity. There were no needy persons among them. For from time to time those who owned lands or houses sold them, brought the money from the sales and put it at the Apostles' feet, and it was distributed to anyone as he had need.

> "… from time to time those who owned land or houses sold them, brought the money from the sales and put it at the apostles' feet, and it was distributed to anyone who had need." (Acts 4:34-35)

We have seen a mystical unity produced by the power of the Holy Spirit, a ministerial unity produced by a decision to fulfill the commission of Jesus, and now we see a material unity which is produced by the love of Christ working within us.

Notice first the spontaneous expression of that unity. In order to provide for the needs of everyone around them, those who had possessions sold them and laid them at the Apostles' feet so that the distribution could be made. As a result, there was none who lacked. This was a spontaneous expression of what God had done in their hearts. The unity they felt, they now expressed by sharing everything they had.

In a different context this may look like communism to some people. But communism breaks down because of the selfishness of the human heart and the ruthlessness of the ambitions of those who seek to impose it on others and enforce it by the use of raw power. What we see here is not communism, it is a spontaneous expression of people who really cared for one another.

We see an expression of people who were more interested in the purposes of God than their own material possessions. This truly is something which was born from within, not something which was imposed from without. They cared, and so they gave. The spirit of what happened here is to be expressed again and again.

This passage is not to be taken as God commanding everyone to sell their possessions and live in a communal society. But He is telling us, quite clearly, that our possessions are only a means by which His work can be accomplished. Everything we own is ours by the grace of God, and we ought to hold it all lightly so that we are able to give gladly if there is a need. That's the real message - a very important message indeed.

You can tell quite a lot about a person's Christian faith by their giving. People who are truly surrendered to Christ reflect their commitment in their giving. When I see people who don't give, or who give very little, or who make excuses as to why they can't afford to give, I immediately know that there is something not quite right in their relationship with God. When a person who has been taught what the Scripture teaches about giving, but then ignores it, that indicates they do not take their commitment to Christ seriously. It indicates that they are not willing to be obedient to God's will for their lives.

If Jesus has your heart, He has your money and possessions too. If He doesn't have everything, He doesn't really have your heart. There are many things that we aspire to do for Christ, which we may not be able to do, even though we have the desire. But one thing all of us have within our power to do is to give.

We have a wonderful example of a man who was a giver. Joseph, a Levite from Cyprus, whom the Apostles called Barnabas, sold a field he owned and brought the money and put it at the Apostles' feet. (Acts 4:36-37). In order to emphasize the nature of what was happening among these early disciples, we are given a specific example of one who knew how to live because he knew how to give.

Barnabas and Paul later join together and become a mighty team as they preach the Gospel all over the region. His name was Joseph - a Cyprian Jew. He was a Levite, one who was devoted to the handling of sacred things. But because of his nature, he had been given a new name by the Apostles. His new name was Barnabas, which meant 'Son of Encouragement.'

Here was a man with the gift of encouragement. Every time you see him in the book of Acts, he is engaging in a ministry of encouragement.

Later on, in the book of Acts, when John Mark defected during the first missionary journey with Paul, it was Barnabas who interceded for him, and eventually took Mark and worked with him. Later on, Mark was used in a great way, perhaps because Barnabas had been his encourager. Here was a man whose heart was toward the Lord. And so, it seems quite natural that he would be mentioned as one who sold his land and gave the money for the church's use. He was an encourager. He was a giver. We need more men and women like Barnabas. We need more encouragers in the body of Christ.

Sadly, not everyone is like Barnabas. In Acts chapter 5, we see the story of two who were not. Ananias and Sapphira pretended to be faithful and committed Christians. They wanted to appear to others like givers. But what they claimed to be true was not a reality in their lives, and they suffered a disastrous consequence. Barnabas is presented to us as a wonderful role-model and his attitude and giving heart had a profound impact on those around him.

What happened in the life of the early church can also happen to us today. We can be filled with the Spirit's power, united in vision, united in purpose, united in our love and concern for one another. We can become people who make a difference in this world, if we are people in whose lives Christ makes a difference. We can enjoy unity of the Spirit, the power of God and effective ministry as we allow Christ to live His life in us and through us.

May it be so, Lord!

CHAPTER NINETEEN
Pass the Salt, Please

"Pass the salt, please." It's a common occurrence at mealtime. I like salt on certain foods. I don't like it because it's pretty, or because it looks good in fancy saltshakers. I like it because it makes my food taste better. It seasons my food. That's why I like salt on some foods. Wouldn't it be a shame to have lots of salt and not be able to get it out of the shaker?

I've been to restaurants where the holes in the saltshaker were too small. How frustrating it is to shake and shake and shake and only get a little bit of salt out. I usually just remove the top and get at it that way. Or we've all had saltshakers that were clogged because of the humidity. It's frustrating to have salt trapped in the saltshaker.

I fear that's where many Christians are today - trapped in the saltshaker. The saltshaker to which I refer here is, of course, the church and the Christian communities to which we belong.

If you bring someone to Christ and give that person about two years, they will probably have so thoroughly disassociated themselves from non-Christians that they literally have no real non-Christian friends. The sad thing about that situation is that many Christians think it is good. Indeed, there are those who would have you believe that to have no non-Christian friends is to fulfil the biblical command to not be "of the world." But the practical result is that we isolate ourselves from opportunities to share Christ. We become salt trapped in the saltshaker. It may be a stained-glass saltshaker, but we are trapped, nonetheless.

In the text I want to look at in this chapter, we see the process by which God greatly expanded the ministry of the early church. It is the process by which God literally shook the salt out of the saltshaker. The central truth of this passage is that the primary business of church ought to be sharing the Gospel with everyone.

This passage begins with crisis and ends with communication. It begins with the disciples in Jerusalem and ends with them being scattered all over Judea and Samaria. It begins with just a few preaching the Word and ends with a multitude sharing Christ. I pray that God will allow us to see the heartbeat of the Holy Spirit when it comes to our own commitment to witness. If we are going to live biblical Christianity in a secular society, we must seriously evaluate that commitment in light of the example we see in the pioneers of the church.

As this text begins, we find the early church still located only in Jerusalem. God had indeed done a great work there and many thousands had come to know Christ. There was nothing wrong with this church. In fact, it was a great church. They were doing what God had called them to do, and that is, to share the Gospel of Christ and to see souls born into the Kingdom of God. But it was still only in Jerusalem. Then everything changed.

> *"On that day a great persecution broke out against the church in Jerusalem, and all except the apostles were scattered throughout Judea and Samaria. Godly men buried Stephen and mourned deeply for him. But Saul began to destroy the church. Going from house to house, he dragged off both men and women and put them in prison. Those who had been scattered preached the word wherever they went." (Acts 8:1-4)*

The salt of Gospel truth had not spread to Judea and Samaria. Initially, the salt had spread out over Jerusalem, but Jerusalem was now becoming a saltshaker in itself. They were in danger of becoming trapped in the saltshaker. How would God move them out? I believe God decided to do something to shake them from the saltshaker. He sent a divinely appointed crisis.

Great persecution came upon the church in Jerusalem and, as a result, they were scattered throughout the regions of Judea and Samaria. I'd like for us to look at three things about this divinely appointed crisis of persecution. First, we need to see that this crisis of persecution was God-ordained. It was all a part of His plan to enable the church to fulfil the Great Commission.

You will recall in Acts 1:8, that Jesus had said, "*But you will receive power when the Holy Spirit comes on you; and you will be my witnesses in Jerusalem, and in all Judea and Samaria, and to the ends of the earth.*" Jesus had said they would begin in Jerusalem, move on to Judea and Samaria, and finally, they would preach the Gospel to the remotest corners of this earth. But the church was still stuck in Jerusalem. God wanted them everywhere. So, God sent this crisis to move them out into the regions of Judea and Samaria.

Just like this crisis, things will happen in our lives providentially. Sometimes God has to nudge us in very strong ways in order to move us into that place of service where He wants us.

Don't ever look on the hard circumstances in your life as having no purpose. I have found that many times God is in those difficult situations, seeking to speak to me about something in my life.

Sometimes we have to remember that God is not interested in our comfort. He is interested in us doing His will and in us being conformed to the image of Christ. God leads us in that way individually and collectively. And here we see the providential timing of this crisis of persecution in the life of the early church.

The second thing we need to see about this crisis is that God had a purpose in allowing this persecution to come upon the church in Jerusalem at this time. The purpose was to scatter His disciples throughout the region around Jerusalem. It says in the first verse that they were scattered throughout Judea and Samaria.

God's purpose was not simply to get them out of Jerusalem. He wanted to get them into other places where lost people needed to hear the gospel. God had a clear purpose for these disciples, and that was to reach people throughout the entire world.

Salt is no good in the saltshaker. Salt is only good whenever you use it, whenever it's placed on food to season and to add flavour. This was all a part of the deliberate plan of God to use the church to reach people for Jesus. He couldn't leave them in Jerusalem while there were lost people everywhere else.

Third, we see that this persecution was preparatory. God called His church to do a great work that could not be done by just the leaders alone. Notice, in this passage of Scripture, just who was scattered abroad. It says all except the apostles were scattered throughout Judea and Samaria. Not everyone was scattered. In other words, the apostles stayed in Jerusalem.

God's purpose was for the church in Jerusalem to share the good news and see people come to know Him. The scattering of that church was preparatory to that work being done on a much wider scale. But the work would not be done by the apostles alone. For the world to be reached, the ministry of the apostles had to be multiplied, not necessarily by creating more apostles, but by all the people becoming proclaimers of the gospel.

Don't miss this point here. If we are going to see people won to Christ; if we are going to reach our world with the gospel of Christ, it cannot be accomplished by the leaders alone. If we are going to reach people for Christ, it will be because every disciple of Jesus becomes active in sharing their faith and winning people to Jesus Christ. They were all scattered except the apostles. The divinely appointed persecution had done its work, and now the church was poised to reap a very great harvest.

We move now from a divinely appointed crisis to a divinely anointed communication. The crisis was intended to move them to communication of the Word of God. Let's look at four things about their communication. First of all it was perceptive. In verse 4 it says, "*Those who had been scattered preached the word wherever they went.*" In other words, since they were scattered, they went about preaching the Word. The early church was perceptive enough to understand that what had just happened to them had happened for a God-ordained purpose.

Like Joseph, they saw that God was in it. In Genesis 50:20, Joseph said to his brothers, "*You meant it for evil, but God meant it for good.*" The early church saw the hand of God in their scattering. They understood that the reason they were where they were now was to share the good news of Jesus Christ.

That is the same perception we need to have. It's amazing how many Christians think they are where they are for some other reason than serving God. You are not where you are because of your job. You may think you are, but that's not why you're here. No, you're not here because of some financial or professional decision you made, you're here to serve Jesus Christ. Those of you who were not born somewhere else, were moved to where you are at present primarily so you could be a witness to Christ in your current community.

You see, in order for Christ to reach the whole world, He has to put His people in the whole world, in all the places He needs a Christian witness. If you are in law, God put you in law to share Christ with others in law. If you are in medicine, God put you there to share Christ with others in medicine. If you are an engineer, God put you there to share Christ with engineers. If you are retired, God has given you are circle of influence among your peers in which you can shine the light of Christ.

Whatever and wherever you are, God put you there to share Christ. We need a Christian witness in every profession, in every occupation and every part of our society. The salt of the gospel needs to be spread over all the world. I remember a Christian tradesman said something many years ago which I have never forgotten. He said, *"I'm not a bricklayer who happens to be a Christian, I am a Christian who happens to be a bricklayer."* Don't ever get those priorities mixed up. The first and foremost priority of every human is to serve God and spread the gospel. The early church was perceptive enough to understand that. Those who had been scattered, preached the word wherever they went.

The second thing we need to see is that their communication was participatory. By that I mean that everyone was involved in it. You will remember it says that everyone except the apostles were scattered. It says in verse 4 that those who had been scattered preached the word wherever they went. If the apostles remained in Jerusalem, then who was preaching the Word? Everyone else! It was ordinary people with ordinary occupations sharing about an extraordinary Saviour.

Thirdly, we need to see that their communication was prolific. In the New International Version, it says that they, *"preached the word wherever they went."* In the King James Version, it says they *"went everywhere preaching the word."*

God called them to begin in Jerusalem, extend the proclamation to Judea, further on to Samaria, and then finally, to the ends of the very earth as they knew it then. The gospel is for everybody, everywhere. They understood that it was not enough to share with one person occasionally. They must share the gospel with every person at every opportunity. The call of the church is to be prolific as we share the good news. We must never be satisfied. We must always be reaching out with new ways, new methods to reach people for Christ.

Then finally, their communication was relevant. It says in verse 4 that they preached the word wherever they went. They were sharing a message relevant to the needs of people and the only message that is pertinent is the gospel of Jesus Christ. When you share with people, don't simply share with them about a book you've read or about the latest fad. You may begin there, but we must at some point move to share with them about Jesus Christ. That's the only thing that will really meet people's needs. It is the old, old story about how Jesus Christ loved them in the midst of their sinful condition, came to this earth, lived a perfect life and died on a rugged Cross for their sins. Share with them how He was buried and rose again on the third day and how He now offers them eternal life and the power to turn from their sin and embrace His gift of eternal life by faith.

We have a high and holy calling to share the gospel of our Lord Jesus Christ. It is both a command and a privilege. But even more than that, it is the news others desperately need to hear. Their eternal destinies depend on it. Like the church in Jerusalem many of us are in danger of staying trapped in the saltshaker. But God is speaking to us and saying clearly that we must break out. We must break out of our comfort zone and take the time and make the effort to get to know people all around us with a view of leading them to Christ.

Now, you may not be an evangelist. God has not called everyone to be an evangelist, but He has called everyone - including you - to share the gospel. How can you fulfil that calling? Well, you may not be comfortable enough with that acquaintance to sit down and share a full gospel presentation with him or her. That's OK. If you can't do that, you certainly can bring them to a place where they will have the gospel communicated to them in a clear and compelling way. You can invite them to join you at a service one Sunday. Or perhaps, before then, you can give them a link to my teaching website and let them begin exploring the truth about Jesus in a less threatening way, at their own pace.

This is what Andrew did when he met Jesus. The Bible says that he first went and found his brother Simon Peter and brought him to Jesus. Andrew didn't know how to share, but he knew where to bring his brother. You too can participate in an 'Operation Andrew' right here and now. You can take the time to identify your brothers and sisters in your circle of influence and bring them to a place where they can hear the good news that Jesus can completely change their lives forever.

God desires to shake us out of the saltshaker. Only then can we be the seasoning that makes a difference in the world. Will you allow Him to use you to touch the lives of others? Don't be trapped in the stained-glass saltshaker. Hear the call of God once more, "Pass the salt, please!"

CHAPTER TWENTY
Seize the Opportunity

Read: Acts 8:1-8; 26-40

It is easy to turn inward and become focused on ourselves. It's only natural. After all, we're programmed that way. All our lives we grow up thinking that we are the most important person we know. We spend our time trying to please ourselves. Slowly, as we mature, we learn that others are important too, and when we come to Christ, and embrace His mission, we should begin to focus on others in a big way.

Yet even Christians can fall into the trap of becoming refocussed on themselves because at the very core of human nature there is a tendency toward selfishness. It's a part of what we call the old nature. It's habitual, and habit patterns are very hard to break. Sometimes it takes powerful forces or events to blast us out of these comfortable patterns. But unless they are changed, we will quit growing.

The early church found themselves in such a situation. They had seen a great move of God in their lives. It had begun at Pentecost, and the church in Jerusalem had become a dynamic church. But the message needed to get out of Jerusalem. Jesus intended for it to be preached to everyone, so God did one of those things that He does when His people get complacent - He shook them up as we saw in the last sermon.

Persecution arose against the church and they were scattered. Only the apostles and a core group stayed in Jerusalem, and those who were scattered went everywhere preaching the Word. God took the salt and poured it out of the saltshaker, where it could do its job. The early church had not lost its desire to share the good news, but it just needed a push to get it out where the people were. The desire to share Jesus should be natural for Christians. If you love Jesus, you want to share Him with others.

The desire is there, but even when God thrusts us out into the marketplace, sometimes the opportunities pass us by. In the hustle and bustle of human life, our encounters with people are often brief and fleeting. We hurl past one another like speeding chariots on an old Roman road. How do we catch those chariots of opportunity? How do we keep those witnessing opportunities from passing us by?

The story of Philip's witness to the Ethiopian eunuch is a story of a divine appointment - of a seized opportunity to share the good news of Jesus Christ. It's the story of how one man caught the chariot of opportunity and led another man to Christ.

The first thing necessary is a searching sinner. In order to lead someone to Christ, you have to have someone who needs to be led. There must be someone who has been prepared by the Holy Spirit. That is essential. Among all the other important elements necessary in the witnessing encounter, two are fundamental. You must have a sinner; and you must have a soul-winner. Whatever the method or program, all have one thing in common - a lost person encounters a saved person, a sinner encounters a soul-winner.

The searching sinner in the text above is the Ethiopian eunuch. It says about him in verse 27, that he was an important official in charge of all the treasury of Candace, Queen of the Ethiopians. Several things stand out about him. The first of which is that he was respectable. He was a court official of the queen. You might say that he was a member of her cabinet.

In the East, eunuchs often attained positions of great authority and power. The text indicates he was in charge of the treasury of Ethiopia. His title could have been Secretary of the Treasury. This was no menial job. We see some indication of his status and prestige in verse 28. It says that he was sitting in his chariot. Very few people could afford the luxury of having their own chariot in those days. This was the luxury BMW or Mercedes of that day. It was his status symbol. Here was a man with a great deal of influence and wealth.

Here was a man with great authority and power. Here was a man with status and prestige. Here was a very respectable citizen indeed. But he was still lost.

It's possible to be the most respected citizen in the community; to be a person of prestige and power, influence and wealth, and be lost and on your way to an eternity without Christ. The Bible says in Romans 3:23, "*For all have sinned and fall short of the glory of God.*"

A person's status, position, prestige, influence, wealth, education and authority do not save them from the consequences of sin. Only a personal relationship with Jesus transfers us from the roll of the lost to the roll of the saved.

We also need to see that this man was religious. In verses 27 and 28 we learn that this man had gone to Jerusalem to worship, and on his way home, he was sitting in his chariot reading from the book of Isaiah the prophet. He was returning from worshipping God in Jerusalem.

Here we have what was known as a Gentile God-fearer. This was a person who believed in the true God, but who had not become a full proselyte of the Jewish religion. Somewhere along the line, he had become convinced that the God of Israel was the true God and so he made a pilgrimage to Jerusalem.

No doubt, he desired to come there and learn the truth about God. I'm sure his heart was eager with anticipation as he set out for Jerusalem. There he can visit the Temple, make his offerings, converse with the Rabbis, walk in the court of the Gentiles, talk to the Priests and Levites. The scholars of the law could explain the finer points of faith to him. Perhaps his position as a court official would provide an open door to the Sanhedrin council. Perhaps he could even get an interview with the High Priest.

So, he set out on his journey. It was a journey of perhaps 1,500 kilometres. He journeyed long up the Nile and then across the desert sands of Sinai, and finally, through the hill country of Judea. Then there it was - the Holy City.

The great walled city appeared before his eager eyes, and there in the midst of the city was the Temple of God, bathed in golden splendour, like a fiery beacon on Mt. Moriah. At last, he had arrived. But his journey was to end in disappointment.

What he would find was hypocrisy, materialism, intolerance, exclusivity and sectarianism. What he encountered was not a living faith, but dead Judaism. And so, the Scripture says that he was returning, sitting in his chariot, reading the Scriptures and trying to make sense of his faith. This is a sad picture of religious humanity without Christ.

The tragedy of our day is that so many people attend religious services yet go home with empty hearts. There are thousands in our country today who have joined a religious organisation but have not actually met Jesus yet. Religion is not the door to a genuine encounter with God, in fact, it is the greatest barrier.

We also need to see that this man was receptive. We notice in verse 28 that he was sitting in his chariot reading the book of Isaiah the prophet. God had prepared this man to hear. He is a searching sinner whose heart is empty, whose life is unfulfilled, but who is receptive to the truth. He is typical of so many today. Often the people we encounter today are inwardly looking for something that's real. They know their life is unfulfilled, but don't know how to find that fulfilment. They're open, receptive and ready for someone to share the truth with them.

They are like this Ethiopian – they're searching. Here was a man who was responsible, but lost; religious, but lost; receptive, but lost. He is like so many of your friends, your co-workers, your neighbours, even some in your family perhaps. What a searching sinner needs is a soul-winner. And that's who this man found in Philip. Philip was one of the first deacons in the early church, but he knew the highest calling of any Christian was to be a soul-winner. So, Philip began to preach the Gospel. We see him down in the city of Samaria, proclaiming Christ to the multitudes who gathered there and revival broke out. People were being touched by the power of God.

What we need to notice about Philip is that he was open to being led by God. In the midst of that great revival in Samaria, he was in tune with the leading of the Lord. He was listening and open to what the Holy Spirit would say to him. In verse 26 it tells us that an angel of the Lord said to Philip, *"Go south to the road - the desert road - that goes down from Jerusalem to Gaza."* Because he was open, God was able to speak to him through this angel, and Philip heard the word of the Lord.

Philip was also obedient. God spoke to him and told him to leave that great revival meeting and proceed to a virtually uninhabited dusty desert road. Philip could have said, *"Wait a minute, Lord, things are going well here. Revival has broken out, the Spirit is moving, people are rejoicing. I'm having the time of my life. I can't go just yet."* But Philip didn't say that. Philip obeyed. If we truly want to be soul-winners, we must be both open and obedient to the word of the Lord and to the leading of the Spirit. If we don't want the chariots of opportunity to pass us by, we must be in tune with the Spirit's leadership and responsive to His call. Philip was, and so he journeyed down this desert road toward Gaza.

Philip was not only open to the leading of God and obedient to the word of God, he was also quite observant. It was on this road to Gaza that he spied a chariot with an Ethiopian eunuch sitting in it, reading the Scripture. Our text says in verse 29, that the Spirit told Philip, *"Go to that chariot and stay near it."* The Spirit directed Philip to the chariot and he discerned an opportunity to share Jesus Christ.

In verse 30 it says that Philip ran up to the chariot and heard the man reading Isaiah the prophet. *"Do you understand what you are reading?"* Philip asked. Philip was observant enough to note an opportunity to share Christ from the Scripture. So, he asked a leading question to get the conversation started. We see the result of this in verse 31. After Philip asked the Ethiopian if he understood what he was reading, the Ethiopian said, *"How can I ... unless someone explains it to me?"* So, he invited Philip to come up and sit with him.

Because Philip was open, obedient and observant, he had caught this chariot and now had an opportunity to share the good news of Jesus Christ. If we want to be used by God to bring people to Christ, we must also be open, obedient and observant. We must be open to the leading of the Lord, obedient to go and share our faith, and observant enough to seize all opportunities to share the good news of Jesus Christ. We cannot afford to pass by or let ourselves be passed by those chariots of opportunity. We must seize every opportunity to share our faith in Christ, and those opportunities only come as we place ourselves in contact with other people.

Notice also that Scripture was involved in this situation. This is not by accident, but by God's design. If we would be effective, we must be prepared to use Scripture to bring people to Christ when God leads us. This Ethiopian eunuch was reading from Isaiah 53, and from that passage of Scripture Philip shared the good news of Jesus Christ.

We must understand that the Scripture is inspired. In short, it's God's book. From beginning to end, it is God's revelation to us. It is inspired by the Holy Spirit. That is why this Ethiopian eunuch was reading it, the Spirit had led him to this passage at this time, the same Spirit who led Philip to come at that very moment and help this brother understand what he was reading.

Secondly, we need to understand that the Scripture is instructive. The Scripture reveals Christ to us. This Ethiopian was reading from the Old Testament, from the book of Isaiah. Christ is the central theme of the Bible, from Genesis to Revelation. In Philip's day, all they had was the Old Testament. The New Testament wasn't written at that time.

So, here in the book of Acts when we see them reading or preaching from the Scriptures, it's from the Old Testament. But they're preaching Christ from the Old Testament. From Genesis through Malachi, Christ is the central theme. The Bible is instructive in that it reveals Christ. It's easier for us because we now have the New Testament which speaks directly of Christ.

Thirdly, we must understand that the Scripture is indispensable to bring people to Christ. When we share the gospel with people, we need to share the Word of God from the Bible. It is the Word of God which has the authority and the power to convict and convince people of their need.

Finally, this witnessing encounter ended with a supernatural salvation coming to this Ethiopian. Salvation is something God does by His Spirit. We can't save anyone. We can only share the good news with them. It is the Holy Spirit's job to convict them of sin, to convince them of their need for a Saviour and to open their heart to the uncredible love of God in Christ. This is what happened to this Ethiopian eunuch.

The first thing that came was conviction. We see the Ethiopian saying in verse 36, "*Look, here is water. Why shouldn't I be baptised?*" They were travelling along that dusty road, Philip was preaching Jesus from Isaiah, the Holy Spirit was moving in the Ethiopian's heart, and now he expresses this desire to come to know this Jesus. God was at work, and the Ethiopian was convicted of his need.

The second thing that happened was confession. In some of the later manuscripts verse 37 says, *"And Philip said, 'If you believe with all your heart, you may.' And he answered and said, "I believe that Jesus Christ is the Son of God.'"* Faith is a matter of the heart. The Ethiopian wanted to be baptised. In other words, he wanted to make a commitment to Christ. He asked if he could, and Philip said, "*If you believe with all your heart.*" The Ethiopian confessed his faith in Christ. He said, "*I believe that Jesus Christ is the Son of God.*" And as Paul tells us in Romans 10:10, "*For it is with your heart that you believe and are justified, and it is with your mouth that you profess your faith and are saved."*

Then finally, we have a commitment. The Ethiopian followed through on his faith and confession and was baptised. Verse 38 says that he gave orders to stop the chariot. Then both Philip and the Ethiopian went down into the water and Philip baptised him. Here was the follow-through.

Baptism is often the first step of obedience. Baptism, in itself, doesn't save anyone. But those who are saved, desire to follow the Lord in baptism. The Scripture says that we are to *"repent and be baptised."* Baptism is an outward symbol of an inward work of grace. It is a public confession of faith, indicating the Christian is willing to live for Jesus. In this act we see the Ethiopian eunuch's commitment to follow the Lord.

In the text, we see this man brought to Christ because of the faithful witness of a sensitive soul-winner. An opportunity was seized by an obedient Christian to share the gospel with a respectable, yet lost man. We see God using His Word to reveal Christ and the Spirit of God working in the heart of someone who was searching for answers. All this was made possible because a searching sinner came in contact with a sensitive soul-winner.

God desires that we all be the kind of sensitive soul-winner that Philip was. This kind of commitment on the part of believers to share their faith in Christ is what made the early church so great. These disciples effectively spread the gospel all throughout the known world because they were believers who saw themselves as ambassadors for Christ and agents of the Kingdom of God.

Now the most famous part of this story comes at the end after Philip had led this Ethiopian to Christ. The Scripture says, in verses 39 and 40, that when they came up out of the water, the Spirit of the Lord suddenly took Philip away, and the eunuch never saw him again, but went on his way rejoicing. Philip, however, appeared at Azotus and travelled about, preaching the gospel in all the towns until he reached Caesarea.

Philip's work was over here and the Spirit snatched him away. The Ethiopian looked around and could not find Philip. But he rejoiced that he had found the Lord Jesus. Philip found himself elsewhere all of a sudden. But he didn't look back. He just kept preaching the Word.

So should we, wherever we find ourselves.

So, the questions before us all today are simple, but confronting:

Are we seizing the opportunities God gives us every day to share our faith and tell others about Jesus?

Are we even looking for those opportunities?

Do we trust God to prepare the hearts of those people to Whom He leads us to share the word of our testimony?

Are we actively praying each day for those divine opportunities where God leads us to 'that' person, like He led Philip to this Ethiopian?

If we can't answer 'yes' to questions like that, then I fear there is only one question before us:

Why are we still here!?

CHAPTER TWENTY-ONE
What's in a Name?

"… and the disciples were called Christians first in Antioch."
(Acts:11:26)

"What's in a name? That which we call a rose by any other name would smell as sweet." These words from Shakespeare's Romeo and Juliet ask an important question, but also imply an interesting answer. The answer Shakespeare assumed is probably the same answer you may find today. Most people, like Shakespeare, would say that there is really not much in a name. After all, a rose would smell as sweet no matter what you called it.

It is said that Abraham Lincoln asked some of his associates an interesting question along these lines. He said, *"If you call a dog's tail a leg, how many legs would the dog have?"* They replied, *"Five."* He said, *"No. That's wrong. The answer is four. You can call a dog's tail a leg if you like, but it's still a tail."* The point is that things are what they are, no matter what they're called. So, what's in a name? Do names matter, or are they unimportant?

Regardless of what Shakespeare thought, or what some people may think today, there *is* much in a name, biblically speaking. As we open the pages of the Old Testament, we find that names are very significant. Names mean something. Here in our text in Acts, we come upon a name by which we are all known today as believers in Jesus. It is the name *Christian.* Our text says, *"And they were called Christians first at Antioch."* What does it mean for you personally to be called a Christian? Do you understand the significance of bearing the name of Christ? Does it mean the same thing to you as it did to those early believers. Is it a badge of honour or an embarrassing insult?

I invite you to consider with me in this chapter what it means to be identified with that holy name. In order for us to understand what it means to be called a Christian; we must apprehend the central truth involved in names.

We must answer the question, *"What's in a name?"* and we must do it by understanding the biblical perspective on names. We need to see that in the Bible, names are symbolic. In Scripture, names have real meaning for the individual. The essence of the person is captured in their name. When God created Adam, He gave him that name because it means *'man.'* Eve was created. Her name means *'mother of all living.'* God brought the animals to Adam and gave him the task of naming them all. I'm sure their names had something to do with their characteristics.

In the Old Testament we see parents choosing names for their children in order to reveal a nature. Jacob was so named because he had his hand on his brother Esau's heel. Jacob means *'heel-catcher.'* His brother Esau was so named because he was red and hairy. Judah means *'praise.'* Samuel means *'asked of God.'* Levi means *'joined in harmony.'* The name Tabitha means *'graceful.'* and Esther means *'star.'*

We also find God changing the names of certain people in the Old Testament. Why did He do this? He did it to show that their lives now had a new direction, a new meaning, a new purpose. Abram was changed to Abraham, which means *'the father of a multitude.'* Sarai was changed to Sarah, which means *'princess.'* Jacob's name was changed to Israel because he was a *'prince with God.'* In the New Testament, Simon's name was changed to Peter, which means *'rock.'* Saul's name was changed to Paul, perhaps in honour of his first convert, Sergius Paulus.

In the Bible, the names of God Himself reveal His character. They show us His nature. He is El Shaddai, the Strong One. He is El-Elyon, God Most High. He is El-Olam, the Everlasting God. He is Jehovah Jirah, the God Who Provides. He is Jehovah Rophe, the God Who Heals. He is Jehovah M'Kaddesh, the God Who Sanctifies. He is Jehovah Shalom, the God of Peace. He is Jehovah Sabaoth, the Lord of Hosts. He is Jehovah Tsidkenu, the Lord Our Righteousness. He is Jehovah Shammah, the God Who is There. He is Jehovah Nissi, the Lord Our Banner. And He is Jehovah Roi, the Lord Our Shepherd.

In Isaiah 9:6 (NASB) it says of Christ that, "*His name will be called Wonderful, Counselor, Mighty God, Eternal Father, Prince of Peace.*" The names of our Lord Jesus Christ abound in Scripture. He is the Second Adam; our Advocate; the Alpha and Omega; the Ancient of Days; the Amen; the Author and Finisher of our Faith; the Blessed and Only Potentate; the Captain of our Salvation; the Chief Shepherd; the Cornerstone. He is the Dayspring; the Desire of the Nations, the Faithful Witness; the First and the Last; the Good Shepherd; our Great High Priest; the Holy One of God; the Great I Am; the Judge of Israel; the King of the Jews; the King of Saints; and the King of Kings.

He is the Light of the World; the Lord of Glory; the Lord of Lords; the Messiah, the Mediator between God and Man; the Man of Sorrows; the Mighty God. He is the Prince of Peace; the Resurrection and Life; the Rock of our Salvation; the Rose of Sharon; the Root of David; the Saviour of the World; the Shepherd and Bishop of Souls; the Son of Righteousness; the Son of Man; the Son of God. He is Shiloh; the True Vine; the Truth; the Witness; the Word of God; the Lamb of God; the Lion of the Tribe of Judah. That's who Christ is.

What's in a name? There is <u>much</u> in a name. Names in the Bible were symbolic. In Scripture, names are also significant. In marriage, for instance, the wife takes the name of the husband. That is because it is a covenant relationship. In taking the name of her husband, she identifies as one with him in this covenant. To call ourselves by a name is to identify our allegiance. We all have family names which identify us. We call ourselves by names to identify our loyalty. When we come to Christ, we are baptised in the name of the Lord. We call ourselves Christians, and so, identify with Christ. Names really do mean something.

The old adage, "*Sticks and stones may break my bones, but names will never hurt me*" is something we try to live by but it doesn't work very well because good names give us a positive self-image; and bad names strike at the heart of who we are. The truth in regard to names is they are both symbolic and significant. They tell us who we are and they identify our allegiance.

So, let's look at this characteristic term appropriated by these early Christians. *"They were called Christians first at Antioch."* Why were they called Christians for the first time there in Antioch? What was it about these early believers that caused this term to be applied to them? *Christian* literally means *'belonging to the party of Christ.'* Some have said that it may have been used at first in a derogatory manner. But in whatever way it was first used, there were good reasons that it was applied and it has stuck.

Something was going on in the lives of these believers. God was at work in their midst. They had been spectacularly born again by the power of God. They were learning to follow Jesus and to be filled with His Spirit on a daily basis. Their lives were being changed and He was the centre of it all.

One of the main reasons why I believe this term was applied to these believers is that they were thoroughly *of Christ*. They were thoroughly *Christian* in word and in deed. Christ was the centre of their conversation because He was the centre of their whole lives. Everywhere they went they spoke of Christ. I'm sure every person to whom they spoke heard the old, old story of how Christ had changed their lives. They were certainly Christians in word, but they were also Christians in deed.

These early believers in Antioch also lived for Jesus Christ. They didn't just talk the talk, they walked the walk! They allowed the life of Christ to emerge in them. These early Christians not only wanted to speak about Christ, they wanted to live for Him. They were conforming their lives to the image of Jesus Christ and this was apparent to everyone around them.

It therefore seemed natural for the term 'Christ' to be applied to these believers. Perhaps those who applied that term desired for it to be a slap in the face. They may have said, *"Why, you people are trying to be little Christs. All you do is talk about Christ. Your whole life is centred around Him. I know what you are. You are a Christian."* But a term which may have been meant as an insult, was one which accurately described their way of life and so it stuck, and they were proud to be called *Christian*.

I can imagine Barnabas running into the church office one day and saying to Paul, "*Paul, do you know what they're calling us now?*" Paul replies, "*No, Barney. What is it?*" Barnabas says, "*They're calling us Christians.*" "*Christians?*" Paul ponders. "*That's right,*" says Barney, "*Christians.*" Paul leans back in his lambskin Lazy-boy and says, "*You know what Barny, I think I like that. Christian. I like that a lot.*" Barnabas speaks up and says, "*Yeah, I think I like it too! It sure beats, 'First Judeo-Apostolic Church of God in Christ International.'*"

"*And they were called Christians first at Antioch.*" Christians – it accurately described who they were. What's in a name? There is much in a name, fellow Christian, for you bear the name of Christ Himself, and there is a vital consideration for every believer in so bearing that name.

One of the Ten Commandments says, "*You shall not take the name of the Lord your God in vain.*" (Exodus 20:7) Were you aware that it is possible for believers to take the name of the Lord in vain? You might say, "*Certainly. Believers can blaspheme and curse too.*" But that's not what I'm talking about. As a matter of fact, I don't think cursing or swearing is what God had in mind when He gave us this commandment. Most people who curse don't even realise what they are saying. I believe it's possible to take the name of the Lord in vain without ever speaking a word. In fact, believers are the ones who are in danger of taking the name of the Lord in vain, not unbelievers. This is a vital point.

We have already seen how there is a great significance in names, that names identify our allegiance. We have seen how those who commit their lives to follow Christ are called by His name. We are called *Christians*. We bear His name as Christians. The Bible teaches that we can be faithful to His name.

> "*I know where you live - where Satan has his throne. Yet you remain true to my name.*" *Revelation 3:8 says,* "*I know your deeds. See, I have placed before you an open door that no one can shut. I know that you have little strength, yet you have kept my word and have not denied my name.*" *(Revelation 2:13)*

We can be faithful to His name. The Bible also teaches that we are judged in the end by the name we hold.

> *"Then I looked, and there before me was the Lamb, standing on Mount Zion, and with him 144,000 who had his name and his Father's name written on their foreheads." (Revelation 14:1)*

> *"No longer will there be any curse. The throne of God and of the Lamb will be in the city, and his servants will serve him. They will see his face, and his name will be on their foreheads."* *(Revelation 22:3-4)*

We are identified with the name of Jesus Christ. How we live our life determines whether we take His name in vain or not. The Bible teaches that we can dishonour His name. His name can be profaned or defiled by our disobedience and our unfaithfulness.

Every believer needs a consistent testimony in daily living. The Bible teaches us that the goal of every disciple is to be conformed to the image of Christ. As we worship Him; seek His face in prayer; study the Scriptures; walk in obedience and faithfulness to Him; as we daily surrender to Him and live in conformity to His will; we will give forth a visible testimony of the grace and presence of God Himself. We will walk in a manner worthy of our calling as Christians. *"And they were called Christians first at Antioch."* We are still called Christians today.

I'm reminded of the story of Alexander the Great. Alexander was a brilliant strategist and a mighty conqueror. He was not only a great leader of men, but he was fearless in battle. Often times, he would charge forth leading his men, riding his mighty horse, Bucephalus. He would hurl himself headlong into the fray and still be standing when everyone else had fallen. He was a very courageous man. There was not a cowardly bone in his body. He conquered the known world of his day and it is said of him that he wept when there were no more lands to conquer.

The story is told of him sitting in judgment on the battlefield. There he was judge and jury. His word was law. When he spoke, it would just be done – no discussion!

There on the battlefield, he would take his seat, flanked on either side by his most trusted officers. Before him would be brought all of those who had charges against them. On many occasions, his judgment would be extremely harsh, especially in those situations involving desertion.

Before him one day was brought this lad, a fair-haired youth and very young. Alexander asked what the boy's name was. The officer presenting him said, *"Alexander, sir."* At once, the great general's countenance softened. It was as if he was flattered that the boy had his name. His men breathed a sigh of relief at that point and thought that perhaps there would be some leniency for this young man, whatever his crime.

Alexander inquired as to the nature of the charges against this young lad. His officer replied, *"Cowardice, sir. He fled in the heat of battle."* The previously soft countenance of the great General was suddenly transformed into an intense, tight-jawed grimace. Looking the boy squarely in the eye, he said to him deliberately, *"Son, what did you say was your name?"* The lad replied, *"Why, Alexander, sir."* Speaking again to the boy, this time in a louder tone he said, *"Young man, what did you say was your name?"* The young man answered in a stutter, *"Why, uh-uh Alexander, sir."* To that answer, the emperor bolted off his throne and grabbed the terrified young soldier and shook him and said, *"Young man, change your behaviour or change your name!"*

Is it possible for us to take the name of the Lord in vain? Might the Lord be saying to us, *"Christian, change your behaviour or change your name?"* Because we have the name of Jesus and are called by that name, we should live in a way which is glorifying to His name. The Lord loves us and will care for us and bless us regardless of our behaviour – but what about all those outside the family of God? When they look upon those who bear the name Christian, will it still be an insult – will it still be a name that is used to deride and attack? Or will our behaviour and lifestyle and witness be such that people see the supernatural power and the Person Who lies behind that name?

CHAPTER TWENTY-TWO
Making a Difference

Read: Acts 16:22-34

There are not too many people who enjoy being different. The idea of standing out from the crowd fills many with fear. We want to blend in and the reward is acceptance and to a certain degree anonymity. We want to be accepted as one of the group, and not stand out like an ink stain on a white shirt!

The only problem with this kind of thinking is that it keeps us from having any impact on anything or anyone. George Bernard Shaw said, "*The world is ruled by deeds, not good intentions, and one efficient sinner is worth ten futile saints and martyrs.*" If we are to live lives that make a difference in the world, we must live lives that are different from the world. We must rise above the average and the status quo like an eagle rises on the wind. That's the picture the prophet Isaiah had.

> "*… those who hope in the LORD will renew their strength. They will soar on wings like eagles.*" *(Isaiah 40:31)*

By God's grace, God's empowering presence, we can be different and we can make a difference in the lives of others. How we act and react in this pressure-cooker world should be important to us because of how it affects us, and because of how it impacts others. The Bible teaches that we are ambassadors for Christ. We are here, in Christ's place, appealing to others to be reconciled to God. If what they see in our lives is a Christian faith which makes a difference, then they will be interested.

But if what they see is the same old thing they see in themselves, they will dismiss us without a thought. In our text today, we journey with two men who made a difference. They would later be called those "*who had turned the world upside down.*" *They* made a difference because they were different. In this chapter, we will see how we can become more like them - how we can become people who actually make a difference.

What happens when a terrible situation becomes the reality of your life? All you're doing is trying to live your life, do your best, do what's right. You're not doing anything wrong. And then, unexpectedly, without warning, you are bowled over by a set of circumstances over which you have absolutely no control. Well, that's precisely what happened to Paul and Silas. They had been preaching the Gospel wherever they were, and now they come to Philippi. But not everyone likes what they are doing or saying.

> "The crowd joined in the attack against Paul and Silas, and the magistrates ordered them to be stripped and beaten. After they had been severely flogged, they were thrown into prison, and the jailer was commanded to guard them carefully. Upon receiving such orders, he put them in the inner cell and fastened their feet in the stocks." (Acts 16:22-24)

Notice how this situation unfolds. Because of their witness for Christ, not because they had done anything wrong, they were both arrested. And the first thing that happens to them is that they are sentenced and beaten. The magistrate conducted a kangaroo court, in which he was judge and jury. Their robes were torn from their backs, and they were beaten with rods. The Scripture says that they inflicted many blows upon them. This would have been truly excruciating. Then they found themselves thrown into prison.

Not only were they sentenced and beaten, but they were also secluded and bound. It was not enough to beat them without a fair trial. Nor was it enough to throw them in jail without determining their guilt. They were thrust into what the Scripture calls the inner prison. This was the most secure dungeon in the prison complex. It was a horrible place. It was a cell, dug deep into the earth, located in the centre of the prison. There were no windows, therefore, no light. The floor was dirt. It was damp. It stank with the odour of human waste. This is a bleak picture indeed. But the picture is not complete … not only were they thrown into this horrible place, but the jailer fastened their feet in the stocks. Even within this inner prison, they were bound with chains.

It would be difficult to describe a more depressing situation than that which befell Paul and Silas. I am sure they could have easily asked the obvious question, "Why?"

There is a truth here which we must understand. The truth is that bad things can happen to good people. If we do not understand this truth, we will be forever asking, "*Why?*" All of us, saved and unsaved, good and bad, will have to deal with bad situations. The Bible teaches that the rain falls on the just and the unjust alike. We all live in a fallen world, and because of the sinful condition of all of humanity, bad things happen, even to good people. It's how we react to those things that will count.

The Devil comes along, like Job's wife did, and says, "*Curse God and die.*" In other words, *"Blame it on God and give up!"* That's what the Devil always wants us to do. He wants us to quit. He would like for us to become convinced that God is not really on our side after all, that it's no use to continue to trust in Him. If we would become discouraged, begin feeling sorry for ourselves, blame God for all our troubles, and throw in the towel, that would play right into Satan's hands. But rather than doing that, we need to do what Paul and Silas did.

> *"About midnight Paul and Silas were praying and singing hymns to God, and the other prisoners were listening to them."* (Acts 16:25)

Rather than bring out the worst in them, this dreadful turn of events brought out the best. Notice, first of all, that they were focused in prayer. In the midst of this dark situation, they had not forsaken God. They knew that what they needed most, only God had. What we see here are men praying in a crisis, but not simply because of the crisis. I'm convinced they were praying because prayer had become the normal thing to do for both of these disciples. Indeed, prayer ought to be the normal thing for a Christian to do in every situation of life, both the good and bad. Prayer is the great privilege believers have of talking over every detail of life with God.

Most of us would pray if we were in as desperate a situation as Paul and Silas, but it would only be a prayer of desperation. God still answers those prayers – but He really desires to have a daily, moment by moment relationship with us - not just hearing from us when we are in a bind. When God sacrificed His only Son to bring His lost children home, He didn't plan to have them run off again and only call home when they ran into strife. So, we need to learn how to pray when times are good or bad. We need to develop a strong daily prayer life, where we learn how to communicate with God and learn to hear His voice. If we do, then when the hard times come, we will be able to effectively touch heaven and receive grace to help in time of need.

Notice also the nature of their prayer. It was not merely a lament over the terrible situation in which they found themselves. Their prayer was a prayer of worship and a prayer of praise. We see here that they were not only focused in prayer, but their hearts were full of worship. The text tells us that around midnight, Paul and Silas were praying and singing hymns to God. Far from being depressed, they were full of thanksgiving! They knew God had not forsaken them; that somehow God was going to do a mighty work in the midst of this terrible situation.

They saw in this obstacle an opportunity. They knew the truth that God manifests His presence in the praises of His people so they focussed on the positive, not the negative. They had become faith-driven optimists. Being an optimist is always a matter of perspective. It depends on how you look at things whether you are an optimist or a pessimist.

Two shoe salesmen were sent to Africa and South America. The pessimist in Africa wrote back, "*I'm coming back home. Nobody wears shoes here!*" The optimist in South America wrote back, "*Great news! Nobody wears shoes here - send me lots more stock!*" It's always a matter of perspective.

The world is crowded with people who look at the negative, always see the dark side and never believe that there is good in the midst of every bad situation. I'd rather be an optimist.

In fact, there is really no option for genuine Christians to be anything but optimists! Sadly, there are thousands of people in the church who are quick to point out faults, barriers, obstacles and problems. They are the first to complain when things don't go their way. It's a sad truth that they exist, but there really is no room for such a person in the church when we read the New Testament. It makes absolutely no sense that a person who is supposedly indwelt by the Spirit of God Himself could view life through such dark, depressing glasses.

The bottom line this this: a pessimist is not only a person who is living in denial – denial of the power of God to meet their every need, they are also living in sin: the sin of unbelief.

When we consistently find faults and deficiencies and problems in people, in life and even in ourselves; when we focus on the things we don't have or can't do and ignore the things we do have and can do, then we are effectively slapping God in the face and saying: *"You are not powerful enough, Lord, to do anything about my sad and sorry lot in life."*

This is the sin of unbelief in action; it's failing to trust God in the most basic areas of life; it's evil; it's destructive to the very fibre of the church; it quenches the Spirit of God in you and those around you; it's a demonic, critical spirit that does not belong in a child of God and when you discern that spirit in yourself or in those around you – it needs to be confronted. Call it what it is – sin! It must be cut out of you and those around you and the church – like a malignant tumour.

A critical, judgemental, pessimistic spirit is just like a rapidly multiplying cancer in the Body of Christ. We tolerate it at our own peril.

Personally, I believe that we have been allowed to whinge and criticise and find fault and complain far too long. We have become so used a fault-finding, negative outlook in us and others that we are no longer offended by it - it no longer seems to worry us like it should.

Paul and Silas were optimists and they had good reason to be. They were optimists because they knew the God Whom they served. They knew what He had done in their lives and they had absolutely no right to complain – not even when they were beaten and bound and thrown into a stinking hole.

These two believers knew that they deserved only death; they deserved the full judgement of God and it is only by His grace and His love and His mercy that they live and breathe. So rather than compare their current situation with what they might enjoy outside the prison – they compared it to death – which is where they were headed before the grace of God transformed them and brought them into the Kingdom of God. They had experienced the wonder-working power of God's love and they lived with the reality of that every day.

We too have experienced that same wonderful God. We serve a God Who loved us before we ever knew what love was; who saved us when we only deserved His wrath; and who has met us time and time and time again with His love and mercy, patience and forgiveness – grace upon grace upon grace upon grace! God has done many miracles in our lives and He will always stand with us in the hard times.

Because Paul and Silas understood this about God, they were full of praise when many of us would be suicidal, angry, fearful and totally devoid of faith and courage. Picture two beaten, bleeding, cold men in the darkest dungeon, at midnight, lifting up their voices in praise to God.

They were singing when they should have been crying. They were rejoicing when they should have been lamenting. They were hopeful when they should have been distraught. They were doing the exact opposite of what the world would do.

Notice also that it says the other prisoners were listening. When you are facing a difficult situation and you have a song in your heart and praise on your lips, those people around you will surely notice.

Too many Christians live as though God is not real. With their lips they may tell you they believe in God, but by their lives they refute their own confession. It is ironic that the church needs to be exhorted to live as though God were real, but that is precisely the exhortation we need. We must live as though God were real because He IS real - and the world needs to hear that truth from us and see that truth in us: God is real!

So, how big is your God? Your lips may confess that He is the Almighty, all-powerful Creator and Sustainer of the Universe and nothing can stand against your God. But what your lips many confess; what your voice may sing on Sunday – could so easily be denied on Monday when your life does not embrace the power of God. Well, in the midst of this dreadful situation, God began to move. Notice what happened.

> *"Suddenly there was such a violent earthquake that the foundations of the prison were shaken. At once all the prison doors flew open, and everybody's chains came loose." (Acts 16:26)*

The whole jail was shaken! God sent a tremendous earthquake. The foundations of the prison were shaken. Get this picture: the shaking was so great that the doors of the prison cells were opened. But we see something interesting here: the chains which bound these prisoners also fell from their feet and hands. This was no normal earthquake. This was the supernatural work of God. God was responding to the worship and prayers of His servants and He shook this prison and set the captives free!

Revivalist, Vance Havner once said, *"When we go through God's testing properly, all we lose are the shackles that tied us up earlier."* Paul and Silas had passed the test. God had heard their prayer. He had received their praise, and now He acted on their behalf.

But notice something else. Not only do we have a shaken jail, we have a shaken jailer. The jailer woke up, and when he saw the prison doors open, he drew his sword and was about to kill himself because he thought the prisoners had escaped. But Paul shouted, *"Don't harm yourself! We are all here!"*

The jailer called for lights, rushed in and fell trembling before Paul and Silas (16:27-29). Not only was the jail shaken, so was the jailer. He had been asleep until this earthquake hit. When he awoke, he saw the doors to each cell were now wide open. He assumed all of the prisoners had escaped. Knowing that the punishment for a Roman guard with escaped prisoners was death, he drew his sword to kill himself.

How surprised he must have been when he heard Paul's voice! He was shaken at first physically by the earthquake; he was shaken even more on an emotional level when he saw the prison doors open - shaken to the point of committing suicide, in fact. And now, when he heard they were all still there, he was shaken to the very core of his being. It says that he rushed in and fell trembling before Paul and Silas. This once proud Roman guard, humbled before his captives. This tough, thoroughly disciplined soldier knew something supernatural was happening.

The amazing thing about this incident is that even though the doors were wide open, and the chains had fallen from them, no one had left. We've already seen how Paul and Silas were praising God in the midst of their imprisonment. Could it be that they had such peace that they felt no compulsion to leave, even when the prison doors were opened? Undoubtedly so.

They were truly men who trusted in God. But what about all of these others? What was it that caused the other prisoners to stay as well? Well, I believe they stayed because Paul and Silas stayed. They had seen something in these two men which they wanted. Their lives had been impacted and changed by a living testimony from Paul and Silas. We can see here the transforming power of God in the heart of a sinner. The first thing this Philippian jailer would receive was a new heart.

> "He then brought them out and asked, 'Sirs, what must I do to be saved?' They replied, "Believe in the Lord Jesus, and you will be saved - you and your household." Then they spoke the word of the Lord to him and to all the others in his house. At that hour of the night the jailer took them and washed their wounds."
> (Acts 16:30-33a)

Because of what he had seen in Paul and Silas, this jailer asked the question of the ages. He said, *"What must I do to be saved?"* Their reply was, *"Believe in the Lord Jesus, and you will be saved - you and your household."* That very night, this jailer put his faith in Jesus Christ and received a new heart. He was a changed man. He took Paul and Silas and washed their wounds. He brought them to his house and they shared the Lord Jesus with his whole family. Something indeed had happened to this man. He had been born again. But notice that he not only received a new heart, he received a new home.

> *"Then immediately he and all his family were baptized. The jailer brought them into his house and set a meal before them; he was filled with joy because he had come to believe in God -he and his whole family." (Acts 16:33b-34)*

Not only he was born again, his whole family was. He received a new heart and a whole new family, all because he put his faith in Jesus Christ. Now he, too, could rejoice in the power of God to save. They had trusted, not in a God who had to deliver them from the hard times, but in a God who would be with them in the hard times. And as a result of that kind of faith, lives had been changed.

Do you see what has happened here? Because of how these two Christians responded to a terrible situation, other people were then impacted for Christ. People were changed because they saw a difference in the lives of Paul and Silas. And they will be changed today, when they see a difference in our lives.

Never apologise for being different. It is in being different that you truly make a difference! We have not been born to blend. We have not been called to be like other people. We have been called to be like Christ. We must allow Christ to live His life in us and through us. It will be a life full of power, full of praise, full of Jesus. It will be different, manifestly different, from the other lives lived out around us.

CHAPTER TWENTY-THREE
Hearing from God

When Jesus spoke of truth, Pilate replied, "*What is truth?*" The question of Pilate is precisely the same question people are asking today, "*What is truth?*" How do you know what is true? Is there absolute truth, that is, truth which never changes? Or is truth relative? Is there truth which applies to all of us? Or are we in the same position described in the last chapter of the book of Judges where it says, "*In those days there was no king (or authority) in Israel; everyone did what was right in his own eyes.*"

Mankind has always been searching for the truth, but as we embrace the reality of the 21st century, forces conspire to make this search meaningless. Some would have you believe that truth is relative. They would say that truth is a subjective thing, that you must find what is true just for you. To them, there are no absolute truths, and if there is no absolute truth, then the search for truth becomes an exercise in futility. Without absolute truth, everything or nothing could be true. And if man, exercising his own limited wisdom, is left to discover the truth on his own, what we call truth is only the collective ignorance of mankind.

If there is no absolute truth, then we have no basis on which to evaluate what we hear. We are besieged on every side by those who would tell us what to believe. How are we to know what is true? There should be a way for the average man or woman or young person to evaluate what is right and what is wrong. Well, there certainly is.

God is the source of absolute truth and we discover that truth as we discover God. He speaks His pure truth to us in a variety of ways. The most obvious and reliable and objective source of truth is God's Word as revealed in the Scriptures, the Bible. The Creator God has provided all of His creation with a record of His dealings with mankind over many centuries, in a collection of written words which were inspired and then preserved by the Spirit of God.

When the Canon of Scripture was finalised and the Bible we now possess was formed, it was decreed by the Church leaders to be *"The supreme standard by which all human conduct, creeds and religious opinions should be tried."* It is this book that stands as the objective test of revelation from God. The Bible doesn't contain all that God has ever said, nor is it the only vehicle for His life changing Word. However, it is the final, objective, agreed upon standard for testing everything that would be presented as the voice of God.

> *"Now the Berean Jews were of more noble character than those in Thessalonica, for they received the message with great eagerness and examined the Scriptures every day to see if what Paul said was true. As a result, many of them believed, as did also a number of prominent Greek women and many Greek men."*
> *(Acts 17:11-12)*

In the above text, we see an illustration of what can happen when people correctly respond to the Word of God. Here we will find several principles which can enable us, not only to discover the truth, but to apply it to our lives. Paul and Silas had been in Thessalonica preaching the Gospel to the Jews there. But some of the Jews were jealous and created an uproar.

They stirred up the people so much that it became dangerous for Paul and Silas to remain there. So, the brethren hustled them out of town in the middle of the night and sent them to Berea. Of course, when they came to Berea, they continued preaching.

They went immediately into the synagogue of the Jews. But the people they found in Berea were of a different calibre than those in Thessalonica. Verse 11 tells us the people in Berea were of more noble character than the Thessalonians. Why were they more noble? The answer to that question is found in the way they reacted to the Word of God.

> *"Now the Bereans were of more noble character than the Thessalonians, for they received the message with great eagerness ..." (v. 11a)*

The people in Berea were more noble because they received the message with eagerness. There was an openness to the Word preached to them. They had an anticipation, an expectancy, that God might be speaking to them. And this is what set them apart. There was a readiness and receptivity to the Word of God. These are the characteristics which made them a cut above those who had just rejected the truth. And these are the characteristics which enabled them to hear from God.

There are many who engage with the church today without the expectation that God will speak to them. Perhaps coming to a church worship service has just become a habit, and so, very little thought is given to why we are there. Or, perhaps because of past experience in a church where the gospel was not fully preached, nothing is really expected. The unfortunate consequence is that generally speaking, when nothing is expected, nothing is gained.

We need to always come into the presence of God and His people with the expectation that God will speak to us. We need to come with an eagerness of mind, with an openness to hear what God would say. If these qualities are cultivated by us, they will place us in a position where we can hear the voice of God.

God most certainly will speak to us, but only if we listen for Him. The still, small voice of the Holy Spirit can be crowded out by the clamour of the many voices of the world flooding our minds. That is why we must give time and concentration to listen for God to speak. We must focus in on Him.

Expectancy can actually be cultivated. It can also be hindered and lost. You cultivate expectancy by spending time with the Lord in prayer as you prepare to hear His voice. I wonder how many of us spend time in prayer before gathering for worship each Sunday. Do we intentionally come before God and ask Him to speak to us as we gather together? If not, why not? If we do pray for our Sunday worship times during the week, then we are more likely to arrive on the day with a sense of anticipation about what God is about to say and do. Our worship services should be a culmination and celebration of a week in preparation.

Think of what is going on in any given worship service and all the preparation which precedes that time we spend together. There is preparation in the planning of the service; preparation in the order of service ; the music, the musicians and singers. The leader has to prepare, as does the preacher and those who pray and those who work the sound system etc. People have cleaned the building and switched on the air-conditioning in anticipation of you coming. All of this preparation takes place to make sure we have a service which will honour God and edify His people.

But there should also be preparation by those who attend. You must prepare yourself by prayer to be in a position to hear from God when you come. Of course, much could be said concerning the need to prepare for our services by also sharing with others, inviting them to church, and bringing them with you. When that is the case, we put these people in a place to meet Christ. Nothing is more exciting in a service than to see people come to Christ. That's one form of preparation that needs to be done more.

At the very least, if you would pray for God to speak to you, then a growing sense of anticipation and expectancy would certainly be cultivated in your own life, and you would be coming to worship with a ready mind and a receptive heart. Then, like the Bereans, you will receive the Word of God with eagerness. Not only did the Bereans receive the Word, they discerned the Word. They received the Word because they were of a ready mind. They discerned the truth of the Word because they searched for it, *"…for they received the message with great eagerness and examined the Scriptures every day to see if what Paul said was true."* (v. 11b)

These Bereans weren't content with just the words of man. The reasoning of mere mortals was certainly not enough for them. They wanted a sure word. They wanted a *"thus saith the Lord."* And so, it says of them, that they searched the Scriptures daily to see whether what they were hearing was true. It seems to me that this is the great need in our society today. People are tired of hearing the conflicting words of so-called experts, handing out so much pop-psychology passing for truth. But it is everywhere, and it is sickening to watch.

For the last few decades now, one of the fastest-growing types of television show has been the talk-show. These shows purport to give us information, truth, if you will, which will be valuable to us in living our lives and sorting out the important questions we face. In these shows, the hosts bounce from one person to another, trying to tap the collective wisdom of mankind. The shows are interesting because we all like to hear what other people think. But are these shows full of truth? Do these shows give us a sure word? Far from it, I'm afraid.

It doesn't really matter what the collective majority are saying or doing. We don't need to ask, "*What are others saying?*" We always need to be asking, "*What is God saying?*" We need a sure word. We must have a way to know what is true. The Bereans knew how to find that sure word. They found it in the Scriptures. They found it as they connected to the discerning power of the Spirit Who inspired the writing and the reading of these Scriptures.

We see that they examined the Scriptures daily. In the King James translation, it says *they searched the Scriptures daily.* The literal translation of that word is that they *sifted* the Scriptures.

That means the Bereans poured over the Scripture, comparing Scripture with Scripture, evaluating the word they were hearing from these apostles against the counsel of God's Word in the Scriptures. That is precisely what we need to do also.

What we see here is a strong statement for the priesthood of all believers. The priesthood of all believers is a doctrine we Baptists hold dear. It affirms several important truths. Firstly, the equality of all believers as priests before God. Secondly, the right of each believer to direct access to God in Christ. And thirdly, the responsibility of each 'priest' to minister to others.

As the priesthood of the believer relates to Scripture, it says that everyone can hear from God through His Word and His Spirit. And that is precisely what we see exemplified in this passage of Scripture. The Bereans searched the Scriptures because they knew they could hear from God.

You see, it doesn't take a theologian or Biblical scholar or high priest or robed Bishop to interpret the Word of God for you. God gives each of us the Holy Spirit to reveal His word to our hearts.

This is why a high view of Scripture is so vital to our faith. Some people would contend that a person's view of the Scripture is not that important. I contend that the priesthood of the believer depends on a high view of Scripture. You see, if the Scripture is not true, from beginning to end, then who will tell us what part is true? If the Scripture is truth mixed with error, then we will need a priestly class to tell us what to believe and what not to believe. Someone once said, *"The liberals who believe the Bible is inspired in spots also believe they are the only ones inspired to tell us where the spots are."*

It is precisely because the Bible is trusted as the final source of truth in all matters of faith, that everyone can read it, confident they will hear from God. Yes, it is a confusing and difficult book to understand and put in perspective – there's no doubt about that. To fully digest the spiritual nourishment of this book one needs some teaching, equipping and help. Confusing or not, this is still the objective standard which all sincere Christians hold to as the truth.

But regardless of how high your view of Scripture is, if you do not read, you will never know the truth it contains! You must want to know that truth enough to read the Bible and search it daily. If you do not, you will either just accept what someone else says is the truth and be led into error, or not hear what God is saying to you in the first place, and thereby fail to fully embrace His plan and purpose for your life.

These Bereans searched the Scriptures daily to discern the Word of God. Verse 12 then tells us that many of them believed as did also a number of prominent Greek women and many Greek men. These people received the Word because their minds were prepared. They discerned the Word because they embraced the truth. They responded to the Word because they received the revelation. They responded because they had received revelation through their study of the Word.

In Paul's letter to the Romans he says, "*So faith comes from hearing, and hearing by the word of Christ.*" When believers encounter the Word of God, the Bible teaches that faith is birthed in our hearts. The process is outlined in this passage in Romans. It begins with the Word. Notice it does not say, "*faith comes by hearing the word,*" but rather, "*faith comes by hearing and hearing by the word.*" The picture is not of simply the believer and his/her Bible. The picture is the believer, the Holy Spirit and the Bible. It is by the action of the Holy Spirit as we read the Bible, that we come to a place of spiritually hearing what God has to say in His Word.

You can hear with your physical ears and never hear with your spiritual ears. You can see with your physical eyes and never see with your spiritual eyes. As you open and read the Bible, or hear it preached or taught, you should prayerfully ask God to reveal and apply His truth to your life. As you do, the Holy Spirit will be faithful to speak to your heart the truth of God's Word. He will apply it to your life. He will give you ears to hear and eyes to see. And as He does, faith will rise up in your heart. You will not only understand the truth of the Word of God, you will be challenged and changed by it. Only then are we enabled to respond to the Word of God like these Bereans.

These Bereans responded to the Word because they received the revelation of God as they searched the Scriptures daily. The reason why they responded was that they were committed to put what they would hear from God into practice.

You see, these Bereans wanted to hear from God so that they could live for God. So many people today want to hear from God before they decide whether they are going to obey what they hear. But they will never hear until they are willing to obey.

You see, there is a moral element involved in hearing truth. Over and over, Jesus would say, "*He who has ears to hear, let him hear.*" Not everyone has ears to hear. Only those who are willing to obey what they hear, can be said to really have ears to hear. In John 7:17 it says, "*If any man is willing to do His will, he shall know of the teaching, whether it is of God, or whether I speak from Myself.*"

A person must be willing to do God's will in order to have the discernment to be able to hear from God. There is a moral element involved in hearing truth. Are you willing to do His will once He has revealed it to you? That is the real question you need to answer today.

Many people want to know what His will is first, to see whether they like it or not. But we must be willing to allow the Word of God, applied by the Spirit of God, to change us into the image of Jesus Christ. But in order for that to happen, we must, like the Bereans, receive the Word with a ready mind; discern the Word because we desire the truth; and respond to the Word because we have received a revelation from God and desire to obey Him.

If we really want to see the power of God in our lives, in our families, in our church, and in our city and beyond, we must proclaim and live by His Word. In His Word is life. In His Word is power. In His Word is light. In His Word is salvation. The good news of God is found here, and we must proclaim it.

Karl Barth, one of the most prolific theologians to have ever lived, was once asked what was the most profound theological truth he had ever discovered. It is said that he thought for just a moment and then replied, "*Jesus loves me, this I know. For the Bible tells me so.*"

This world-renowned Bible scholar; this theological giant; the writer of '*Systematic Theology*' – the highest selling theological textbook in history; this intellectual and academic guru regarded the opening line of a children's hymn as the most profound theological truth ever discovered!

Unlike many Biblical scholars, Karl Barth had encountered the living, dynamic, life-transforming, personal God in His Word. May we be committed to doing the same in our desire to hear from God and know the truth. We will never see the sleeping giant wake up if God's people cannot or will not actively seek His face and listen for His voice, each and every day!

CHAPTER TWENTY-FOUR
Becoming Who you Are!

Insecurity is a crippling condition. Yet, it is a plague which has spread throughout all sectors of our society. But this plague is not limited to non-Christians. It affects Christians as well. Our own insecurity as believers keeps us from living a full and free Christian life. As believers, we can be severely retarded in our development because of our own insecurity. Because we doubt our own worth before God, we are all too willing to be content to live a passive Christian life. Because we lack confidence, we also lack the aggressive boldness which we need in order to have a real impact on the world for Christ.

Waking the Sleeping Giant is as very appropriate title for this series in the book of Acts. If the Church of Jesus Christ were to become in practice what we know it is in theory – it would make Godzilla look like child's toy! The church would tower over all of man's wisdom and intelligence and be the central, driving force of society.

The challenge to you and to me is to wake up to who we are in Christ. It is a challenge which every Christian faces on a daily basis as he or she endeavours to be the kind of man or woman God intends for them to be.

Those of us who struggle seriously with the claims of Christ for our lives are constantly challenged with our own need to be more effective in our Christian walk and witness. But sometimes our own fears, doubts and insecurities get in the way of what we desperately desire to do for Christ and who we desire to be in Christ.

How can you be all that you desire to be for Christ when you see so many areas of lack in your own life? Is it possible to be the kind of Christian witness you need to be when you are still struggling with so many shortcomings in your own life? It is true that you can't give what you don't have.

But it is also true that our perception of ourselves is not always accurate. Our insecurities arise, in large part, because we haven't seen by faith and accepted by faith God's own word concerning us. There is a desperate need in the body of Christ for believers to come to know who they really are in Christ. We need to understand God's opinion of us. We need, by faith, to come to know what we have received in Christ. And we need to accept the extent of His forgiveness and acceptance of us.

Our text speaks to this theme by directing us to one who was far from perfect, but who lived in the confidence of his position in Christ. Perhaps as we look at Paul's appearance before King Agrippa, we will not only come to understand his motivation to see people come to Christ, but we will also catch a vision of who we are in Christ which will give us the same confident assurance which Paul had.

> *"At this point Festus interrupted Paul's defence. 'You are out of your mind, Paul!' he shouted. 'Your great learning is driving you insane.'*
>
> *'I am not insane, most excellent Festus,' Paul replied. 'What I am saying is true and reasonable. The king is familiar with these things, and I can speak freely to him. I am convinced that none of this has escaped his notice, because it was not done in a corner. King Agrippa, do you believe the prophets? I know you do.'*
>
> *Then Agrippa said to Paul, 'Do you think that in such a short time you can persuade me to be a Christian?'*
>
> *Paul replied, 'Short time or long - I pray to God that not only you but all who are listening to me today may become what I am, except for these chains.'" (Acts 26:24-29)*

As this episode in the life of Paul unfolds, we find him imprisoned in Caesarea. Because of a near riot in Jerusalem and a plot by the Jews to kill him, Roman officers had brought him to Felix, the governor, so that his guilt or innocence could be ascertained. Paul remained in prison under Felix for two years, at which time Festus succeeded Felix as governor.

During this time, Paul preached the gospel to both Felix and Festus. But neither one of them could decide what to do with Paul. They both knew that he was innocent, yet they wanted to please the Jews, who wanted Paul in jail. They were in a political dilemma. Should truth prevail over political expediency? It should, but very often it does not.

King Agrippa arrived to pay a visit to Festus. Herod Agrippa II was the great-grandson of Herod the Great, who had murdered all the male children in the vicinity of Bethlehem because he feared the birth of Jesus. He came to visit Festus with Bernice, who was sister to Drusilla, Felix's wife. This made her a sister to Agrippa II. We have here a sordid affair indeed. Paul was brought before Agrippa to present his defence.

One characteristic which is unmistakable about the apostle Paul is that he was an aggressive, confident soul-winner. Everywhere he went, and to everyone he met, he gave a witness of the grace of God and of their need to come to Christ for salvation. This meeting with Agrippa certainly was no exception. Picture what must have happened.

> *"The next day Agrippa and Bernice came with great pomp and entered the audience room with the high-ranking officers and the leading men of the city. At the command of Festus, Paul was brought in. (Acts 25:23)*

Great ceremony and pomp surrounded this official occasion. No doubt, Festus had donned his scarlet governor's robe for the special event. King Agrippa and Bernice were also arrayed in the splendour of their royal robes.

I'm sure the court was majestically decorated also. The captains, centurions, and legionnaires stood in stately splendour as they lined the great Hall of Audience to remind everyone who was there of the military might of Rome. The honoured guests and dignitaries looked also witnessed the questioning by Agrippa. Paul is then brought into this magnificent hall, before these imposing earthly powers.

Paul is a man small in stature and physically unimposing. The chains of his imprisonment dangle from his wrists. He wore no royal robe, but rather the robes of a prisoner. Yet, within this little Jewish man is a power unmatched by all the regalia which now surrounds him.

As you look into his eyes, you see a certain majestic confidence and a depth of understanding which was unsurpassed. When Paul speaks, his voice cuts through the pretentious elegance of this glorious display of pomp. What he says rings with truth and is clothed in power.

So, Paul begins to make his defence before Agrippa. But as you read his defence, you find that it is as much a testimony to the gospel of the grace of God as it is a defence of his innocence.

Paul was neither impressed by Agrippa nor afraid of Roman power. Paul was a soul-winner at heart. His motivating desire was to see people come to know Jesus Christ, and so he was determined to use every opportunity to see that happen.

There is a clear message here for us. We see that Paul seized the opportunity to share Christ with Agrippa. The example of Paul should be an encouragement to us to do the same thing. Do we see, as he did, that whatever the circumstance of our encounters with other people, they are opportunities to share the good news of God's amazing grace? When people encountered Paul, they encountered Christ's ambassador, and when they encounter us, they also encounter Christ's ambassadors.

> "*Therefore, we are ambassadors for Christ, as though God were entreating through us; we beg you on behalf of Christ, be reconciled to God.*" (2 Corinthians 5:20)

As ambassadors for Christ, we all stand before this watching world, in the place of Christ, entreating all those who do not know Christ to be reconciled to God. We should use every opportunity we can to get that message across.

We also see an unmistakable message here. It is the message that we must share with every person, regardless of their place in society. Paul preached to the poor, Gentile, and Jew alike. But he also preached to the affluent and socially important as well. Paul could stand before paupers and kings. It didn't matter to him, and it shouldn't matter to us. A man is a man regardless of his title, and without Christ he is lost. Sometimes the temptation is to draw back from sharing with so-called VIP's. And, in our insecurity, sometimes we draw back and miss the opportunities God provides.

What we need is to catch the confidence which Paul manifested here. We need to see ourselves as ambassadors for Christ. We are set forth in His authority and by His command. Furthermore, we possess His power to get the job done. He has ordained us to be His representatives in that confidence. We need not fear any human. We see in Paul an aggressive soul-winner and that is precisely what we can be and should be every day.

What was the effect of Paul's witness to Agrippa? We see that this passionate soul-winner produced a rather anxious King. As Paul preached about the truth of salvation by faith in the risen Christ, King Agrippa was getting more nervous. Agrippa knew of these things, and Paul's testimony had a ring of truth about it. You see, truth produces conviction. And Agrippa was feeling that conviction. Truth will also produce confrontation – every time - and so this was a very tense moment.

Perhaps Festus noticed Agrippa's uneasiness. Because when Paul's message was being driven home, Festus intervened. At this point Festus interrupted Paul's defence. *"You are out of your mind, Paul!" he shouted. "Your great learning is driving you insane."* (Acts 26:24). But Paul would not be turned aside from his goal.

Still standing before King Agrippa, he replied to Festus, *"I am not insane, most excellent Festus," Paul replied. "What I am saying is true and reasonable. The king is familiar with these things, and I can speak freely to him. I am convinced that none of this has escaped his notice, because it was not done in a corner."* (Acts 26:25-26)

Then Paul delivers a call for decision. He says, "*King Agrippa, do you believe the prophets? I know you do."(v.27)* Paul was calling for Agrippa to make a decision. Truth demands a response. Agrippa had already experienced the conviction of truth. And now, he must decide what he will do. He must respond.

Agrippa decides to take the course of evasion. He says, in verse 28, "*Do you think that in such a short time you can persuade me to be a Christian?*" The thrust of Agrippa's statement was that Paul shouldn't expect Agrippa to make such a decision on the spur of the moment.

The fact is that Agrippa was very uncomfortable. He had heard the truth, and somehow, deep down, he knew it to be true. He was feeling the pressure. Perhaps within his troubled heart, faith was attempting to be born. But he quickly aborted that attempt.

In our witnessing encounters we are certain to run into our own Agrippas. Not everyone is willing to hear the truth. You will witness to people who profess to be open-minded, thoughtful intellectuals, but who are opposed to the truth. They will not admit it. Many times, they will seek to evade the truth by refusing to admit it is the truth. They do not want to admit that they are rejecting truth. That would portray them as being not so smart after all. The real reason they reject the truth is not for intellectual reasons, however - it is for moral reasons. There is no other explanation for why intelligent people would reject truth.

The Bible calls this original sin. It is the utter moral depravity of humankind. We are addicted to selfish sinful pleasures and we do not desire to change. This was the situation with King Agrippa. What Paul says next is simply amazing. This nervous King was about to hear a most audacious statement from the lips of the apostle Paul. In response to Agrippa's bold statement, Paul makes a statement of his own.

> Paul replied, "*Short time or long - I pray God that not only you but all who are listening to me today may become what I am, except for these chains.*" (Acts 26:29)

On the surface, I find this statement utterly amazing. What I find incredible is not Paul's desire to see the king saved, but the way Paul expresses that desire. He said that he desired that the king and everyone else *"may become what I am."* On the surface, this seems like reckless arrogance on the part of Paul.

Did Paul think he was such a great person that they should desire to be like him? Why didn't he say that they should become like Christ? After all, isn't Christ supposed be our example? Isn't His life the life we are to emulate? What does Paul's statement say about his own self-worth? What does it say about his view of himself as a sinner who has been forgiven? What does it tell us about Paul's view of the grace of God working in his life?

Paul certainly knew all his shortcomings. He knew his faults. He was acutely aware of his sins. On several occasions in the New Testament, he reminds us of just how great a sinner he was before his conversion to Christ. Paul had persecuted the church. Because of his activity, many in the early church suffered and even died.

I'm sure the apostle spent many hours after his conversion in utter remorse over the pain and suffering he had caused so many innocent saints of God. I'm sure he repented in dust and ashes over his behaviour which had been motivated by a false zeal for his religion. Paul called himself on one occasion, *"the chief of sinners."* He was fully aware of his own sinful past. But he was aware of something else as well.

At just the right time in Paul's life, Jesus Christ had come to him. He had encountered the grace of God. With his face to the ground, he had received Christ as his Saviour and Lord. All of those horrible sins he had committed were forgiven. His heart was cleansed and he was set free. Paul had come to understand the complete forgiveness of Jesus Christ.

He Himself wrote about us and said that we are *"accepted in the beloved."* This sinful man had come to understand that when Christ receives you, *"old things are passed away; behold, all things become new."*

This is perhaps one of the hardest lessons to learn in the Christian life. I know intellectually about the forgiveness of Christ. And I know what the Scripture says about my forgiven state. But while I know that Christ has forgiven my sins, sometimes I find it extremely hard to accept the fact that I am forgiven. I suppose we all find it hard to forgive ourselves, to really believe that we are accepted by Christ. Therein lies our insecurity and our lack of confidence.

So when Paul said that he wished that all those who heard him that day, "*may become what I am, except for these chains,*" we was saying, "*This is my only exception ... I would like for you to be just like I am, except for these chains.*" We, like Paul, must also make some exceptions. What would your exceptions be?

If you had to tell someone you'd like for them to be just like you are, what would you have to except? Would you have to say, "*except for this sin in my life*" or, "*except for this lack of obedience to Christ?*" What would we have to except? All of us have those exceptions, things which we carry like heavy baggage through a busy airport. By the time we get to where we're going, we're exhausted.

The exceptions are burdens too heavy to bear. But in Christ, the exceptions can disappear. In Christ, we can be made whole. In Christ, we can find a confidence for daily living. For we can find acceptance as His children.

Our insecurity flows from the fact that we live in the exceptions rather than the acceptance of Christ. It is hard to forgive yourself, but you must. For Christ has already forgiven you, and you are now a new person in Christ. You can begin again. This is what the grace of God is all about. God knew what He was doing when He chose you. He knows ll about your sins and your weaknesses. He called you while you were in your sin.

The Bible teaches that "*while we were yet sinners Christ died for us.*" The Word God begins, God finishes. Remember that "*you are His workmanship.*" He will see you through by His grace.

If we want to meet the challenge of living biblical Christianity in a secular world; if we want to see the *Sleeping Giant* wake up, if we want to see the Church of Jesus Christ take her rightful place in the world then it must begin here, in our own hearts. We must begin to see ourselves from Christ's perspective. That is why Paul could be so bold and so confident – because he knew who he had become in Christ. We need to know that too.

We are forgiven, cleansed and redeemed by the blood of Jesus Christ. God sees us through the finished work of Christ. We are priests in the Kingdom of God. Regardless of the circumstances which surround us and at time engulf us, we can hold our heads high. We never have to know shame again. We can proclaim the truth of the gospel boldly, seizing every opportunity to share it with every person, everywhere.

The same confidence which we observe here in Paul, can and should be our confidence, because we are indwelt by the same Spirit and we worship the same God!

CHAPTER TWENTY-FIVE
Kingdom Living

As I conclude this study in the book of Acts, I want us to look at the last two verses of this instruction manual for the church.

> *"For two whole years Paul stayed there in his own rented house and welcomed all who came to see him. He proclaimed the kingdom of God and taught about the Lord Jesus Christ - with all boldness and without hindrance!"* (Acts 28:30-31)

Here we see two emphases in the preaching of Paul. At the close of the book of Acts, we find that the apostle Paul preached the kingdom of God and taught about the Lord Jesus Christ. In other words, Paul preached both the Kingdom and the King. So, I want us to explore Kingdom living in this final chapter.

We are living today in a time that some have described as the post-Christian age. By that they do not mean that Christianity has ceased to exist, but that our culture no longer thinks that Christianity is relevant as a way of viewing the world. How we view the world is called our worldview, and we are no longer living in an age that has a Christian worldview.

What scares me, however, is that I am starting to wonder whether we have lost a Christian worldview in the church as well. It is so easy for the world to infiltrate the church. All that is required is for Christians like us to become complacent in our commitment to significant time in prayer, serious study of the Scriptures, generous giving of their resources, and consistent giving of ourselves in the fulfilment of the mission of Christ.

When our attention to those basic disciplines of the Christian faith is lost, we will end up with a sleeping giant. We end up with a Church that, although it's the most significant human organisation on earth, its power is quenched, its glory is lost, and its effectiveness is minimal. We can forget the truth that we are citizens of another Kingdom.

When our highest devotion and deepest commitment is given to the priorities of this earthly kingdom, we end up with a watered-down Christianity in which people know neither the Scriptures nor the Lord Jesus and they are therefore unaware that there is another view of how they should live their lives which is diametrically opposed to the worldview which surrounds us.

The early Christians with whom we have connected in our study of the book of Acts were, without question, counter-cultural in their mindset and their actions. They had come to understand the reality of the rule of the King. There is indeed a King whom we as Christians are called to follow. Our King is Jesus Christ, and His Kingship implies a Kingdom. We call it the Kingdom of God or the Kingdom of heaven – both terms in the bible mean the same thing.

Now, you may not have spent very much time this past week thinking about the Kingdom of God but let me assure you that the Kingdom of God is worth thinking about. Because not only does the Kingdom of God have something to do with how we live in our contemporary culture, it has everything to do with the practical affairs of daily life. It has everything to do with how you deal with your employer; how you provide for your family; how you raise your children; how you treat your spouse; how you spend your money; how you act in the community .. and the list goes on. For Jesus Christ, the Kingdom of God was a priority.

The Bible teaches us that Jesus' message was primarily about that Kingdom. Jesus "*went throughout Galilee, teaching in their synagogues, preaching the good news of the kingdom, and healing every disease and sickness among the people.*" (Matthew 4:23)

The message Jesus preached was the message of the Kingdom of God: "Repent, for the kingdom of heaven is near." (Matthew 4:17) After His resurrection, Jesus appeared to His followers "over a period of 40 days and spoke about the kingdom of God." (Acts 1:3). In fact, over eighty times in the Gospels alone, Jesus refers to the Kingdom. The Kingdom of God is certainly a priority for Christ. Therefore, it cannot be overlooked by us.

It seems to me that not much attention has been given to the Kingdom of God in many of our churches. Perhaps this is due to an incomplete understanding of the mission of Christ and the comprehensive plan of God.

Perhaps the absence of this emphasis is also due to our current emphasis on the practical, organisational aspects of church life. We highlight our structure and programs, sometimes without the counter-emphasis of strategy and purpose. But we not only need to understand *how* to do it, we need to understand *why* we do it. The why is found in our understanding of the Kingdom.

In this final chapter I want to look at the message of the Kingdom and its King so we might gain a genuine *'kingdom consciousness.'* It is my prayer that, as a result of this chapter, and I trust this whole book, you will not only come to an understanding of what it means to be a part of the Kingdom of God, but that you will also begin to see that being a part of that Kingdom is supposed to impact and define every area of your daily life.

We need to understand what the implications of the Kingdom of God are for our life. In order to do that, we must first define what the Kingdom of God is. Most simply stated: The Kingdom of God is the dominion or reign of the King. The Kingdom of God is not limited to a place, or a people, or even a time. The Kingdom of God is defined by the King and His reign. Wherever you find the reign of Jesus Christ, the King, there you will find the Kingdom.

The first thing we need to see is that the Kingdom of God is the cosmic plan of God from the beginning. The Kingdom is what God had in mind before we ever showed up. It is His plan for the entire universe. We only see things in a very limited way. We see the here and now. We see everything from an earthly point of view. We see the physical world as it current exists. But God sees everything from an eternal dimension. He sees not only the physical, but the spiritual. He sees the past, the present and the future. God sees the comprehensive cosmic plan that He has been working out from eternity past. This plan brings together all things in Christ.

The Kingdom rule and reign of Jesus Christ will be the only reality one day. Only His Kingdom is eternal. The kingdom of this world has a use by date! The Kingdom of God always His 'Plan A' and there never was or will be a 'Plan B.'

We have already seen that the message of Jesus was the message of the Kingdom of God. He preached *"Repent, for the kingdom of God is at hand."* But when it came to establishing an earthly expression of that Kingdom, He established the Church. Is the Church the Kingdom of God? No, the Church is not the Kingdom of God. But the Church is an expression of the Kingdom. The Church is a manifestation of the Kingdom on earth. The Church is the catalyst God uses to establish His Kingdom on earth. So, to understand Kingdom living for today, you must understand what God had in mind for the Church.

The Church is the community of God's people, and it is God's desire to manifest His Kingdom through that community. While the manifestation of the Kingdom can be seen wherever you see the rule of Christ, it is God's design and desire that the Church be that body of people to which He can point and identify as the community of the King. Jesus called the Church into existence for this purpose. It is the Church gathered and the Church at work through which we see the Kingdom of God expressed in our world each and every day. Or at least, that's how it is supposed to be.

Are you a part of the Church gathered? Are you a believer in Jesus Christ, who has identified with a local church where you live? Are you committed to that church and actively involved in its life and ministry? Are you involved in the local community of God's people, known as the local church? I hope you are catching a sense that I am speaking about more than just organisational affiliation here. When I ask you whether you are a part of the church, I'm not asking whether you have your name on a roll. I am asking whether you are a true believer in Jesus Christ and have not only identified with a local church but also become involved in the life of the church through your active participation and commitment to that community of faith.

If you are a member of the local church in that sense, then you are also involved in the Kingdom of God, because the Church is the place where the rule of the King should be manifested more than anywhere on earth. He who is the King of kings and Lord of lords is also the Head of the Church, which is His Body. It is through the church that the visible manifestation of the rule of God can be seen. It is through the church that we should hear God speak clearly. It is through the church that we can be organised to do His work. It is through the church that we can be nurtured, discipled and held accountable. It is through the church that we can learn how to minister in Jesus' name. We are the community of God's people. We are part of the Kingdom.

If I was asked *"What on earth is the Kingdom of God?"* I would have to say that at the very centre of that Kingdom you will find the church Jesus birthed and promised to build. That church is the hub of Kingdom activity. From this hub, many other ministries can go forth. But primarily, it is the church on earth which is the most visible expression of the Kingdom of God.

I said before that the church is not only a manifestation of the Kingdom of God, it is also the agent to bring about the Kingdom of God. It is only when we see clearly our mission to spread the gospel of the Kingdom, and engage in committed action to that end, that we are truly engaged in Kingdom work.

God has called us, as the church, to impact the world for Jesus Christ. We are to spread the news that the King has come and is coming again; that He rules by divine rite; and that humanity needs to choose to come under His dominion. We must proclaim this in all that we do. We must infiltrate our society at every level and become involved with people in a multitude of ways in order to get this message across. We must act as agents of the Kingdom of God. We are on a divine mission for God and we must never lose sight of our real purpose.

While we are not secret service agents, in one sense we are still 'under cover.' You must come to understand that your true identity is as an agent of the Kingdom of God.

Your occupation may be one thing, but you are really something else. You may be a lawyer, but you are really an agent of the Kingdom. You may be a doctor, but you are really an agent of the Kingdom. You may be an engineer, but really you are an agent of the Kingdom. People may know you as a corporate executive, but in truth, you are an agent of the Kingdom. To some, you may be a nurse, a housewife, a mother - but to God you are an agent of His Kingdom. When we get to heaven as our final destination, we are not going to be doctors, nurses, lawyers, teachers, accountants, engineers, housewives or even pastors. But we will still be followers of the King.

We therefore need to understand that we are actually involved in Kingdom ministry through the local church. We do not act alone but are part of a community of redeemed people seeking not only to be changed by the impact of the reign of Christ in our lives, but also to make a difference in the world by the proclamation of the rule and reign of Jesus Christ. In order to see the implications of the Kingdom of God, we must understand the importance of Christ being the central focus of that Kingdom.

In the Scriptures, Christ is revealed to us as the Head of the Church. God has centred all things around His Son, Jesus Christ. He is revealed to us in Scripture as the King of kings and Lord of lords. Christ is the centre of all of God's purposes, and all things are to be summed up in Him. The reign of God is exercised through Jesus Christ. He is central to the Kingdom and the church. We need to see the priority of Christ as King.

The Bible teaches us that "*in Christ all the fullness of the Deity lives in bodily form.*" He is "the head of the body, the church." Christ is revealed to us as the divine, sovereign God. It is His rule to which we must submit. Jesus Christ is our top priority. The church is His church, not ours. While we have the privilege to participate in giving financially to support the church and its ministries, to build buildings and establish ministry programs and function in the many ways which we do, we must never lose sight of the undeniable reality that Jesus Christ is the head of the church.

Too many church fellowships lose sight of this reality and begin to function as if they were simply a democracy. But a democracy is the rule of the people. The Kingdom of God, however, is a theocracy. This theocratic rule is expressed through people, through anointed, called and gifted people, but however this is organised, whatever leadership structure we adopt, what we should always be seeking is the will of God. We must always seek an submit to His rule and reign as the King!

Now, not only is Christ the priority for our lives, but in a very practical way, we must live out His rule on a daily basis. This is where it really counts. This is where the Kingdom is expressed in the lives of God's people, and that all comes down to the depth of our relationship with Him and our submission to His leadership and Lordship. Our service for Christ can never be any greater than the depth of our relationship with Him.

The church serves Christ best when we are all thoroughly revived, renewed and submitted to Him. If we need to pray for anything in our day, it is for a thorough revival to sweep across the church; for a great awakening such as occurred under John Wesley, George Whitfield and Charles Finney.

On a practical level, as we begin to see ourselves as agents of the Kingdom and begin to put Christ first in every aspect of our lives, then we will also begin to grapple daily with what it means to live under the rule of Christ. As we do, we will find that we start to live from that perspective. Our actions will reflect Christ's rule and this will mean some real changes in our priorities and how we spend our time.

When Jesus gave us that model prayer, that we refer to as the Lord's Prayer, He showed us a very important priority for our whole lives, not just our prayers. The prayer starts with worship: Our Father Who art in heaven, hallowed by your Name. Our lives should have worship as the highest priority. Our love relationship with our God – our time with Him in prayer and worship and intimacy should be at the top of our list. And after worship, what do we have?

We have the most powerful prayer ever to leave our lips and the highest calling ever to grip our hearts, *"Your Kingdom come, Your will be done on earth as it is in heaven."* That's what it means when we ask for the Kingdom of God to come.

When Jesus came to earth, He ushered in the Kingdom of God. In one sense He left heaven to come to earth, but in a very real sense He brought heaven with Him. You see in heaven we have the rule and reign of Christ manifested totally and completely. The fullness and totality of the Kingdom of God exists in heaven. So, when we pray *"Your Kingdom come,"* we are asking God to release the reality of heaven on earth. We are asking that what is true in heaven will become true on earth. We are calling upon God to release the fullness of His kingdom reign on earth as it is in heaven – right here and now. *"Back up the truck, Lord, dump a load of heaven right here in my church community; right here in my family; right here in my workplace; right across this city and this nation, Lord. Let what is real in heaven be real here!"*

Is that what you really want? Do you think that is possible? Do you know what Jesus was saying when He said we could pray such a prayer? This is kingdom living - when the rule and reign of Jesus Christ overflows from the Kingdom of heaven and saturates this hell hole we call earth! That's what happened when Jesus came. That was one mighty overflow of kingdom power. Satan and his demons went wild. There was warfare everywhere as the manifest rule and reign of Christ set millions of people free. The blind could see; the deaf could hear; the lame could walk; the lost were found; the sick were healed; the lonely were comforted; the outcast were made priests in the new order; heaven came to earth!

Do you understand that this is God's plan and purpose? Do you understand that when Jesus came to earth, the kingdom of God came with Him and since that day the kingdom of God has been forcefully advancing against the kingdom of darkness and will one day totally eclipse this evil kingdom so that there is only one Kingdom in this universe – and that is the Kingdom of light and life and love and peace!

Do you realise that when you utter those words, *"Your Kingdom Come,"* that this is what it really means?

Will there be any sick people in heaven?
Will there be any lost people in heaven?
Will there be any lonely people in heaven?
Will there be any hurting and bereaved people in heaven?
Will there be any pain or doubt or fear in heaven?
Will we experience loss or grief in heaven?

'No' to all of the above! Everything is perfect in heaven and as heaven invades earth, everything will state to change here! Everything that sin and rebellion brought into our lives will just start to disappear. That's the best news of all.

We don't need to wait till we get to heaven to enjoy the glory and the wonder of God's Kingdom. Heaven is coming to us! Jesus brought heaven with Him. Jesus ushered in the rule and the reign of the King on earth, as it is in heaven. Then He left us with the mission to continue bringing the reality of heaven to earth.

When we connect with the plan and purpose of God and realise what is happening here, it should change our whole life! *"Your kingdom come, Lord . . . Your will be done here, now, on earth, in my life and church and relationships, as it is in heaven!"*

That prayer should be on our hearts and our lips every waking moment. We should be consumed by a passion to see more and more of heaven and less and less of the hell Satan has unleashed in this world.

I have nothing to offer you. I have nothing for the pain and agony that surrounds us in this world. When I sit with hurting and grieving and lonely and confused and sick people, I can only do one thing, I can only lift my eyes to heaven and say, *"More, Lord! More, Lord. May Your kingdom come Lord . . . here . . . now . . for this hurting brother or sister. Come, Lord Jesus, and manifest your rule and reign in their life and their circumstances."*

O how we need God in these last days. O how we need Him to wake us up, to wake the Church up right across this nation and around the world! The world needs to see the beauty and majesty and glory and power of the Bride of Christ. We really need the reality, the riches and the power of heaven to explode across the face of every relationship and every ministry and every church fellowship and every government. It's time! It's way over time!

So, whose side are you on? Are you content to sleep away your time in the Kingdom until you get to heaven and get the biggest shock of your life? There are going to be so many of us that cannot believe our eyes or ears when we get to heaven. The difference from this life to the next will be so huge - we will be in a state of shock, I'm sure. But is it not meant to be that way!

Jesus brought heaven here over 2,000 years ago through His life, death and resurrection. That abundant, eternal wonderful life was for now, not just for later. How crazy would it be to lock away the power, glory and life-changing wonder of heaven in the afterlife while His whole creation slips into darkness!

Look around you in this world. There's pain and sickness and doubt and fear and evil abounding and it doesn't have to be that way! The church of Jesus Christ needs to wake up to the truth that we are agents of the King and we already possess the keys to heaven! We no longer need to listen to Satan when he tries to convince us that this is just the way the world is; this is as good as it gets!

When we start praying for the kingdom of God to come more and more; when we start living like the Kingdom of God is already here; when we confess the ugly, horrible sin of unbelief and start taking God at His word … then hang on to your hats people!

The sleeping giant is awake, and the church will finally stand up again and be heard and seen. The King will truly reign. Our world will start to see what Paul's world saw as the rule and reign of Jesus Christ is re-established over His creation.

I don't want to wait until I leave this earth to taste the glory and power of heaven. Why would we ever think we had to wait? Read the Gospels! Listen to the words of Jesus. Look again at what He preached and how He lived and what He released on earth. Look at the birth and explosive growth of the church in the book of Acts. Then cry out to God, day and night and ask Him to wake the sleeping giant and release His Kingdom on earth, as it is in heaven!

How then shall you live in light of what you have read in this book? I believe all of heaven is on the edge of their seats, waiting to hear your answer! And the Holy Spirit is poised and ready to empower the choices you make from this day forward.